# MARIE PONTONNIER

~

# MONTRÉAL PIONEER

An historical, biographical novel by

Carol Ann P. Coté

ISBN-13: 978-1500881986

ISBN-10: 1500881988

# DEDICATION

This book is dedicated to
The Holy Spirit,
who has guided me since childhood.

# Contents

v

# CHAPTER 1   THE NEW WORLD BECKONS

The only thing I could do for my dear friend was to stitch her body into her blanket and watch her slip slowly into the pitch black, frigid water below.

Our ship captain blessed Marguerite with Holy Water and sent yet another of his passengers to the sea with these words: "Dear Father in Heaven receive her soul into Paradise. May all the souls of the faithful departed rest in peace. In the name of the Father, the Son, and the Holy Ghost. Amen."

Our Captain had graciously permitted me to join him on deck for this simple ceremony. I thought she would appreciate my seeing her off to her ocean resting place. He usually prefers to "bury at sea" in the dark of night alone. I really needed to show her how much she has meant to me. For you see she offered to serve as chaperone for me on our voyage across the ocean. Marguerite was a recent widow with no children or living relatives in France. She wanted to make a fresh start in New France and leave painful memories behind.

First she exchanged letters with my paternal cousin Jean Valiquet dit Laverdure, who crossed to the New World three years ago with Le Grande Recrue of 1653 with 104 other soldiers. They were recruited from all over France to help protect Ville-Marie (Montreal) from attacking Iroquois. He is very concerned for my welfare because I'm only thirteen years old. He warned us how very difficult the trip would be.

My dearest Papa passed away last year and my Mama died when I was only six. This was my best chance to find a good husband and have many beautiful children in the New World – New France. Sounds like a dream come true to me. I figured what did I have to lose? I could gain a great deal! What did I have to fear? My sweet Jesus is always with me. We are the best of friends. I know He doesn't want me to become a nun. That was the only alternative for me if I stayed in France. I'm an orphan with a rather meager dowry. Arranged marriages are the norm. Representatives from New France have been actively recruiting "all good girls, aged twelve or over," to come to Canada, marry and have lots of children. It is a Roman Catholic colony. In fact you have to convert to Catholicism before you can board the ship.

I need to introduce myself. I'm Marie Pontonnier. I was born and baptized on the twenty-second of January 1643 in the Parish of Saint – Vincente in Le Lude (arrondisement of La Flèche) diocese of Angers, Anjou, France. My father's name was Urbain Pontonnier and my mother's name was Felicité Jamin. I'm five feet tall, and have dark brown eyes and hair. I confess I'm quite vain about my hair since it is thick and long with a slight wave.

This is the spring of 1656. France has won the war with England! Our territory was returned to us by the Kirke brothers two years ago. And we have signed a treaty with the Iroquois Indians! So it's clear sailing ahead. All that's left for me to do is cross this interminable sea. In the beginning I suffered from sea sickness. I'd never even taken a ride on a boat since Anjou is not on the water. So this was a problem I had not anticipated, but should have.

I'm quite an optimist, so I'm always looking on the bright side of things. No amount of warnings and rumors circulating throughout France of the dangers of Canada: the bitter cold and the Indian raids could have prepared me for the appalling conditions below deck of the one hundred-fifty ton ship named Taureau.

# CHAPTER 2    IN THE BOWELS OF THE BOAT

We are packed like sardines down below in the belly of the beast. Chickens, pigs and cows share our dirty sleeping quarters. Modesty prevents me from disrobing since privacy is non-existent. Delightful smells waft through on the smoke of the lanterns. The scent of the latrine buckets competes with the odor of the barnyard animals. I actually do appreciate the necessity of the animals to provide us nourishment on our trip. I'm sure some of them are destined for the New World also.

Needless to say I spend as much time as possible during the day, good weather permitting, topside, where fresh breezes billow the sails. The lighting is good for embroidery and reading my prayer book. Of course I spend a great deal of my time praying to my Jesus. He helps me see the beauty in the world He has created, instead of dwelling on the discomfort of this journey. All that clean salty air helps me sleep right through the night below in our fetid sleeping quarters. I'm well aware that one out of ten of us will not survive the trip. This vessel is a barely ventilated breeding ground for disease. An "undetermined fever" took my friend. She suffered all without complaint until Jesus came to claim his devoted servant. She'll remain a sterling example to me until the day I die. But I'm determined that my dying day will be in New France, surrounded by my children and grandchildren in my old age, on dry land.

I'm young and strong so I'll make it across this forbidding sea.

We have been experiencing frequent spring squalls popping up out of nowhere. One can easily be swept out to sea by the roiling waves if you aren't careful. All in all this is quite an adventure – dangers above and below. Who knows what awaits us on the other side of the sea. It must be better than the life aboard this boat!

I have made a new friend here who is heading for Québec City. Catherine is eighteen and has as high hopes as I.

My cousin Jean wants me to join him in Ville-Marie. But of course he has not had the good fortune to marry yet. The odds are very rough for men. There are three men to every one woman. So it would not be proper for me to stay with him. I am going to lodge under the care of Mademoiselle Jeanne Mance who is a nurse and administrator of the hospital in Ville-Marie. Papa would approve.

I decided not to sign a "marriage contract" sight unseen before I left for the New World. I'm brave but not that foolish. My cousin has an intriguing candidate in mind for me who is from a very good family. His name is Pierre Gadois. He is twelve years older than I. His father was the very first settler of Ville-Marie. He received the land grant from Governor Maisonneuve in 1648. Pierre became the first altar boy in Montréal. He has learned worthy trades. He is a master armorer, gunsmith and farmer.

But I want to keep my options open and not marry in haste. I want to be sure before I make my vows. Marriage is for life in our Holy Roman Catholic faith. "What God has joined together let no man put asunder." This is the best thing for the couple but especially for their children.

## CHAPTER 3   OH HAPPY DAY!

We woke up to wonderful very welcome news from the Captain. We are on course to make it to the New World in forty days, a personal best for him. Thank you Jesus, for favorable winds aloft. So there are only five days remaining, barring unforeseen problems.

The night before last we bucked a terrifying storm. We had to hold on for dear life below while trying to tie everything down. Our ship sprung a leak which doused our bedding quite thoroughly! It has finally dried out in the bright afternoon sun today. So Catherine and I are dragging ours back down. Thank you Lord for all blessings, great and small. We are all glad we are almost there since our food supplies have dwindled. We are forced to get by on those dreadful hard biscuits, completely devoid of taste.

It's sad to think that Catherine and I will have to part once we reach Québec City. I will have to transfer to yet another boat for the ride up the St. Lawrence River to Ville-Marie. We have promised to correspond of course. I'm heading to the frontier. I guess that makes me a pioneer! Just enduring the voyage on this ship should qualify me for that distinction. "What do you think of your little girl, Papa, all grown up and heading into the unknown? I know you can hear me because I feel your presence all around me. You give me strength. My sweet Jesus, dear Mother Mary and Saint Joseph, Mama and Papa all together in Paradise, bon nuit! (Good night!)"

# CHAPTER 4    LAND AHOY!

It is the fifteenth day of June 1656. Catherine and I have spent the better part of the day with our eyes locked on the horizon. Like Noah of old we await the first bird venturing out to greet us.

It is hard to grasp the fact that I will never see my homeland of France again. When we left it really hadn't occurred to me. I guess the prospects ahead of me squeezed the realization out of my mind. The past forty days and nights have steeled my heart to this conclusion. I will alight on a new land and embrace its challenges. Am I a gambler? Perhaps I am.

I don't know when the boat to Montréal departs, but Catherine has invited me to stay with her in Québec City until that time. What a relief! We are not ready to say goodbye just yet. She has made arrangements to lodge with the Ursuline nuns until she finds a proper husband. I do hope the convent has room for one more beleaguered soul.

At last our seabird vigil has borne fruit! Not just one lonely bird, but hundreds of seagulls are swooping in glorious abandon above and all around us. Raucous "Hurrahs" resound which don't seem to faze them in their glorious flight. As our first glimpse of New France creeps slowly into view, chills of pure unrestrained joy propel my soul up to join them in the heavens. Through tears I pray "Thank you, Jesus, by your grace we have survived!"

# CHAPTER 5   WARM WELCOME IN NEW FRANCE

I am afloat on the water once again after having spent a delightful week recuperating from our ordeal. The nuns could not have been kinder to us. They are quite used to the influx of girls and are praying constantly for our safe passage. Several of them have made the trip more than once and are actively recruiting us to come and fulfill our "destinies as Mothers of New France." They were sorry to know that we made the crossing without their help. They've promised to pray for my dear departed friend and chaperone, Marguerite, who did not survive to see our new land.

I had the very good fortune to meet the "Living Saint" Mother Marie de l'Incarnation. She founded the monastery and school for the education of young girls in 1639. She told us the story of how they struggled to finally build their monastery and school only to watch it burn in 1650. A few hot coals from the fireplace were mistakenly left in a wooden dough trough to help the bread rise. From that tiny source the entire complex burnt to the ground. She was able to throw most of the monastery records from the second floor window to the ground. She barely made it out in time. Then she and her sisters, many in bare feet since everyone was in bed at the time, stood on the frozen ground in the snow and sang the "Magnificat." No lives were lost. The next three weeks they spent with the settlers and

10

eventually were reduced to begging. But with the help of grateful settlers, Indian parents, and Our Blessed Mother they were able to begin rebuilding in 1652, in spite of the fact they were still deep in debt from the original buildings.

So that is why we had a place to stay and good food on our arrival four years later. I had a difficult time tearing myself away from their love and hospitality. One dear Sister accompanied Catherine and me to the wharf where my transportation awaited. I don't have many bags to haul around. I'm traveling light but my heart is heavy at having to part from Catherine. She is like the big sister I never had. I know we will see each other again.

## CHAPTER 6   MY NEW HOME – VILLE-MARIE (CITY OF MARY)

My heart is beating faster and faster as the dock at Ville-Marie pulls slowly into view. There are many more crates of provisions aboard this boat than people. I've been sitting on a wooden box for the three hour trip. It has been a beautiful ride on the Saint Lawrence River on a clear golden day. The shore has been in sight all the way. What a verdant lush land this is! There are fish swimming along beside us. So many I feared one might leap onto my lap. I guess there will always be fish to eat. I'm glad I like them.

There is quite a bustle at the docks as I disembark carefully. It seems we are expected. The big ship, the Taureau, brought much anticipated shipments for the colony from France, supplies which will help to carry us through the fall and bitterly cold winter ahead. This will be quite an adjustment for me. I'll need to make or acquire some warmer clothes quickly.

I'm surprised and delighted that Mademoiselle Jeanne Mance, my guardian, has come to greet me with kisses on both cheeks, which I warmly return. She is a busy nurse who has taken the time to come down to the dock. I'm greatly relieved to find her so sweet and welcoming. She has the kindest face. I feel at home already. "Thank you Jesus! You have reminded me once more that I must learn to trust you in all things."

Mademoiselle Jeanne Mance is excited that a "Get to know you" social has been planned for the church grounds on Sunday afternoon. Our enthusiastic marriage eligible soldiers will be there in force. The spring and summer seasons are when the ships bring us, but this year only ten girls are expected. Most of them are headed for Québec and Trois Rivières. I am the one and only "fille à marier" (marriageable girl) that they expect to come to Ville-Marie this whole year! Oh dear, this prospect is at once thrilling and terrifying. Just how many men will there be jostling for my attention? I hope to see my cousin Jean Valiquet there so he can properly introduce me to Pierre Gadois.

Now I must figure out what to wear! Not that I have that much from which to choose. I'm sure I'll be able to make myself presentable, not that the soldiers will really care. I wonder if they wear dress uniforms for these occasions. I also wish to find a friend around my age. I already miss Catherine. I know she is very anxious to marry very soon since she is eighteen years old. She is so sweet and pretty. I'm sure she'll be saying her vows before the summer is over. I hope to attend her wedding whenever it is. I sure do wish she was here to bolster my confidence while facing the contingent of soldiers. Oh, we humans worry too much about things over which we have little control. Hopefully the weather will cooperate and it will prove to be a sunny Sunday. I'm in no big hurry to marry which relieves some of the pressure on my side. Now the lonely men are quite another story!

# CHAPTER 7    DECISIONS, DECISIONS!

How do I choose the right man with whom to spend the rest of my life? This will not be an easy task. There are a few excellent prospects, among so many, that have risen to the surface.

There's Pierre Gadois, my cousin's choice for me. Tall, handsome, strong and charming—he merits a few stars. I think he would also be a good father and provider. Our personalities fit together so well. He has the most delightful sense of humor, which is high on my list of requirements. My optimism could thrive with a man who can make me laugh. A mutual sense of Joie de Vivre may be essential to thrive in this land full of uncertainty. Yes, Pierre buoys me. He makes me feel secure. Every woman needs that whether she wants to admit it or not.

Now we turn to René Besnard dit Bourjoly, a corporal of the garrison. He regaled me with the most fascinating true story of his harrowing journey with Le Grande Recrue of 1653 (The large recruitment). Ville-Marie was in dire need of fortification so M. Paul Chomedey de Maisonneuve went to France to enlist at least one hundred men to protect the town's perimeter. If he was not successful he would be forced to abandon the attempt to even continue the settlement at Ville-Marie. Two years later he returned with one hundred-five out of his one hundred-fifty original recruits who had signed contracts before notaries with the Company of Montréal. These brave men came from all over France: from Picardie, Champagne, Ile de France, Normandie, Anjou and Maine. They were scheduled to depart in the spring of 1653. There were several delays, but they were so happy to finally set sail on June twentieth upon the "Sainte-Nicholas-de-Nantes" under the command of Captain Pierre le Besson.

Not far out they realized that the ship was in very poor shape and leaking badly. Mercifully the captain gave up trying to proceed and turned the ship to retrace the three hundred-fifty mile trip. He was afraid some of the men would not venture back out once they arrived home to France, so he decided his best recourse was to put them on an island from which there was no escape. They all prayed fervently he would return very soon. On July twentieth a more reliable ship picked them up and they resumed their voyage to the New World.

They landed at Québec on September 22, 1653 after sixty-four days at sea. Governor de Lauzon refused to let them have the necessary boats to complete the journey to Ville-Marie because the vessels were sorely needed to defend Québec! The weary men finally arrived at Ville-Marie on November 16th, just in time for the first icy blast of winter to greet them. Their five month ordeal was at an end.

Yes, René is very brave and oh, so gallant! But there is something about him that concerns me— something underlying the shiny veneer that he is so careful to present to me.

There is yet another Pierre tugging at my heartstrings. He was also with Le Grande Recrue of 1653. His full name is Pierre Martin dit La Riviere. He is an interpreter and surgeon from Anjou, my hometown, so we have that in common. He is very intelligent and erudite, definitely my superior in brain power. We are a good match even though he is much more introverted and serious than I. I enjoy the challenge of enticing him out of his shell. Yes, this Pierre is definitely on my short list.

Oh my goodness, I have a most pleasant puzzle to solve. How do I choose only one from such fine gentlemen? This pursuit will occupy my mind and heart for the near future, while I go about my duties helping Jeanne at the hospital where I'm staying. I'm anxious to help in any way I can. This is an invaluable learning experience that I'm sure will come in handy when I wed and have a family. I have so very much to learn.

# CHAPTER 8   OUR ENGAGEMENT IS OFFICIAL

This was the easiest puzzle I ever worked. Pierre Gadois makes my heart sing! We both know that we are the missing pieces to one another. It's been ten months since I first set foot on this land. Enough time has passed for me to come to the sound conclusion that he's the one. I'm more assured of it as every day passes.

It is time to make this decision official. It is May 6, 1657, a bright beautiful spring day and we are on our way hand in hand to Notary Jean de Sainte-Père's office to sign our marriage contract. Our dear friends Jeanne Mance, Barbe de Boulogne, wife of the fourth governor of New France, Major Lambert Closse, Pierre's dear parents and sister Roberte and my cousin Jean have all gathered to witness our signing and wish us well. We filled Jean's office to overflowing so his mother has asked us all over to their home for tea and fresh baked pies.

Pierre teased his superior Major Lambert that he would be next if he could just get Élizabeth Moyen to give him a second glance. We'll pray about that. This festive occasion has turned into an engagement party we will always remember, a crucial milestone in our lives crossed. I am so thankful for the warm embrace of Pierre's family. They have welcomed me into their fold so I now feel I once again have a family on this earth. How good is our Lord!

# CHAPTER 9   DELIVER US FROM EVIL

Oh, dear Lord! Corporal René Besnard dit Bourjoly is not taking my rejection of him well at all. He is not the gentleman I thought he was.

Pierre and I have decided to set our marriage date for three months from now, August twelfth, to allow René a cooling off period. This will also give me plenty of time to prepare properly for the happiest day in our lives.

I'm enraged that René has sworn revenge on Pierre, threatening to cast a spell over us, at the church during our wedding ceremony! He has vowed that he will carry this out by knotting a cord three times secretly in our presence. This curse will cause us to be sterile unless the cord is unknotted!

If René thinks that this evil threat will cause me to change my mind about him, he is delusional! Pierre is so shaken by this whole development because he comes in contact with René on a daily basis in their work at the fort. He is making his life miserable.

This should be a joyful, carefree time for both of us. I am so afraid that his rage could turn violent. He is proving himself to be quite unstable. He frightens me.

We have consulted with our priest how best to handle this. He has instructed Pierre to recite the Miserere Mei Deus (Psalm 51) backwards in Latin at our marriage ceremony. We are familiar with this antidote since it is the custom back in France to dispel curses. Our priest says Satan despises Latin. This remedy consoles me just a little. To reinforce this I have asked the nuns at the hospital to pray to protect us from this evil looming over our special day and future happiness.

Now for some happy news: Our "marriage contract signing day-engagement party" has brought Major Lambert good fortune. His fondest hopes have been realized. Élizabeth Moyen has said "Yes" to his marriage proposal!

Pierre wondered how I would feel if we were to share our most special day and have a double wedding with them. Absolutely, if they don't mind risking having their day marred by the threat of this curse, it would be fantastic to be with them! Élizabeth and I are very close, and we have many of the same friends. Somehow this relieves some of the pressure on us from René's threat. Maybe he will think better of cursing our marriage in the presence of his superior officer and his bride who are marrying during the same ceremony. Certainly he wouldn't want to have his curse extend to them also.

How nice that we have another "engagement party-marriage contract signing" to attend. We are thrilled to spread the joy. How I wish the whole world could feel the happiness that Pierre and I are lucky enough to have found. I'll enjoy sharing the planning for our double wedding with Élizabeth.

# CHAPTER 10   TEARS OF SORROW MIXED WITH GLADNESS

Élizabeth Moyen is sixteen years old, two years older than I. She and I sat down for a heart-to-heart talk today over a pot of tea. I asked how she and Major Lambert met. She paused a long while before answering as her bright blue eyes welled with tears. Her soft answer shocked me. He rescued her and her younger sister Marie from an Iroquois massacre in which her mother and father both perished, and their home, her father built, burned to the ground. Lambert saved her just four months ago. They had been captured by the Onadaga. Lambert found us half-starved and terrified and brought us to the Hotel-Dieu where Jeanne Mance helped us to recover.  She admits to feeling guilty planning her wedding while she still mourns for them. That awful day is seared into her heart like a red hot poker. It has been hard to visualize a future for herself. Her mind was numb at first, then haunted by the vision of their horrific passing. Now she worries mightily that her magnificent warrior, who has survived so many Iroquois encounters, will one day have his luck run out. How could she bear to be left all alone again? She constantly prays for his safety and that they will be blessed with children very soon. A family to cherish will help her heal. This is what her parents would want for her: happiness.

I am glad that she feels safe enough with me to unburden her soul. This is my first heart wrenching exposure to the real danger we face here in the frontier of New France. The fragility of our situation has been graphically brought home to me. How many tears will be shed in our lifetimes as we forge this new land? Only God knows, and this is a great blessing. If it's His will we shall prevail and our little colony will grow.

Her revelation has left us both emotionally exhausted. So we will begin our wedding plans tomorrow. I decided to ask Pierre's mother Louise to join us. Unlike us, she must have some experience with weddings! She invited us to her home to work it all out.

Louise is such a dear lady, so loving, patient and kind. She volunteered to make my wedding gown, for which I thanked her profusely since my hand sewn seams are not as straight as they should be. I'm sure I'll improve with more practice. I've brought some lovely old lace and ribbons from my mother's things which I put away years ago. I hope we can incorporate them into my wedding dress.

I was forced to sell my beautiful wedding armoire (hope chest) when I left France. It broke my heart since my father had taken great pains to hand carve it for me. He proudly presented it to me on my twelfth birthday. I've been embroidering some linens right along for my trousseau which I did manage to salvage and bring along.

Élizabeth, a much better seamstress than I, plans to make her own dress. We decided to both wear pure bright white. We learn that weddings are all about abundant flowers and food. In mid-August the fragrant asters are in full bloom in vibrant shades of purple, pink and white. Marguerites (daisies) should still be around. I hope so. That would be so perfect, as if Marguerite was still with me in a special way. We will fill in the bouquets with wildflowers, especially those delicate lacy white ones that run rampant in the fields. We'll fill containers to overflowing to flank our Lord's tabernacle on the altar, and tie bouquets to each pew down the aisle. We'd also like to place arrangements on each side of the four prié dieus (our kneelers) and more flowers and ribbons tied to the backs of our four chairs. We will need two bridal bouquets and boutonnieres for our grooms.

Of course many flowers will be required for the wedding feast tables which will be outside on the church lawn under the shade of the trees.

We'll have a morning Nuptial Mass so we can eat around noon, before any chance of summer afternoon thunderstorms, hopefully. There must be music and dancing and plenty of both. Our church has a wonderful fiddler.

Now what food should we serve? Pierre's mom suggests that we should have a buffet of smoked ham, pate chinois (a meat pie made with pork, corn and potatoes), peas and carrots, smoked salmon and crusty wheat and rye breads. For dessert my new favorite, tarte au sucre (sugar pie made with maple syrup, butter and dried fruits) and sucre la crème (like fudge) made with maple or brown sugar or both. Yum!

Now we both need to get our guest lists together, so we can plan for enough food and cooks to prepare it all. My fondest hope is that my shipmate, Catherine Camus, her husband, Charles Gauthier and their first baby, a girl they named Anne, who was born April ninth, will be able to join us. I was correct about Catherine's desire to wed quickly. They were married only six weeks after we landed in Québec! By the time I found out, it was too late for me to attend. We haven't seen each other since I left for Ville-Marie.

Neither couple are inviting Corporal René Besnard dit Bourjoly. He is still simmering with rage and has publicly stated he fully intends to carry out his infernal curse. Father Pijart says there is no way to prevent him from entering the Church since all Masses are open to the public. I apologize to Élizabeth for this black cloud hanging over their special day and thank her once again for her moral support. We part sharing a few more tears and a reassuring hug.

# CHAPTER 11    OUR WEDDING BELLS PEAL!

I know many brides experience doubts and fears the day of their wedding, but I'm not one of them. I'm extremely excited, but not scared one iota. I've found the perfect man for me and I'm so very thankful to God to have found him. I will admit to not sleeping very well last night, with the threat of the evil spell hanging over us. I've tried so hard to dispel the specter of this curse which threatens to intrude on this wonderful day and our future lives. We've prayed constantly to Our Lord for His almighty assistance. Pierre has his Miserere Mei Deus Psalm, which he must recite backwards memorized. He will pray this to himself during Mass. I'm so sorry that this has to distract him from our Nuptial Mass. It is a very long Psalm. I tried to memorize it, but soon realized that I'd be too nervous to carry it out.

I decided for my part I will present my bridal bouquet to our Lady at the end of Mass. There is a lovely statue of Mary to the left of the altar. I will plead at her feet that René's curse will have no effect on us. I will ask for her help to always be a good wife and mother for our children.

I know full well that both my parents smile sweetly down upon us from their home aloft, but oh, how I miss them today! I fasten a wreath of small white flowers on my head and leave my hair long and flowing half way down my back, because Pierre prefers it that way. I place the finishing touch around my neck–a small gold cross I received from my dear Papa on my First Communion Day.

There is a knock on the door. It's Pierre and his family and many of our friends (a French tradition). They are all here to escort me to the church accompanied by musicians. How happy we all are as we walk the short distance to the church from the hospital where I've been lodging. We make up quite a joyous wedding procession. It's a splendid late summer day, August twelfth, 1657. We meet up with Élizabeth and Major Lambert's procession not far from Notre Dame Church. It's debatable whose procession is more jubilant! Father Claude Pijart, our celebrant, greets us on the church steps with a wide smile and outstretched arms. He suggests that all the guests with the exception of the families process into the church. After a few moments musicians lead, then the brides, Élizabeth and I, both orphans, walk in side by side, followed by the family members, and at the end of the line Lambert and Pierre escorting their mothers.

No one notices Corporal René Besnard dit Bourjoly as he stealthily sneaks into the back pew a few minutes later, by the side door, his dark agenda unchanged.

In juxtaposition to him is the church, glorious with lush flowers and candles glowing, all the family and friends in their finest attire, wishing only good things for the happy couples. Here is pure evil straining to overcome the Good in the House of the Lord.

No human being can fully comprehend the supernatural grace that pours down upon us as we receive the Sacrament of Holy Matrimony. The Catholic Church places this wondrous event during the Nuptial Mass. Just as Christ is One with His bride, the members of the Church, Pierre and I become one body, one flesh never to part as we pledge our sacred vows to each other. During Holy Communion we will receive the Body and Blood of Jesus first, and then the congregants. In this Holy Sacrament of the Eucharist, we receive the Body, Blood, Soul and Divinity of Jesus truly present under the appearances of bread and wine. This is God's gift of Love to us. He humbles Himself in such lowly substances for our sanctification. Our God is pure Love so our whole lives should be dedicated to learning how to love Him and others as He loves us. "Dearest Jesus please help me learn through my role as wife and mother to love you as I should."

After a period of prayer in Thanksgiving after Holy Communion, Father Pijart blesses both couples with a special Nuptial blessing and then blesses the congregation. Before we process back down the aisle as husband and wife, Élizabeth and I take a few minutes to place our bouquets at Mary's feet and kneel to pray for her help as new wives and future mothers. We both let the happy tears flow as we each turn to grasp our proud grooms' hands and lead all our friends and families down the aisle and through the church doors into the blinding summer sun. We pause to share our first kiss as husband and wife. We then hurry across the church lawn to the welcome cool of the shade trees, and form an informal receiving line where we are smothered with hugs, kisses and good wishes. The wedding guests include quite a few dignitaries: Governor Maisonneuve; Marguerite Bourgeoys; Marie de Boulogne, wife of the former Governor of New France; Louis d'Ailleboust de Coulogne; Notary Bénigne Basset; Notary Jean Saint-Père; Charles Lemoyne; Maturin Langevin, Sieur de La Croix and his wife Marie Renaud*; Jeanne Mance, my guardian and dearest friend; Marie Moyen, Élizabeth's sister; Catherine, her new husband Charles Gauthier and their one year old baby, Anne. I'm so happy they could come by boat from Québec City. Francoise Bernard and her husband Morin Janot dit La Chapelle; and their baby Cecile; Jean Tavernier dit La Forest, who taught Pierre the trade of gunsmith; Pierre's parents, Pierre Gadoys, and Pierre's mother, Louise Mauger*; Pierre's sister Roberte Gadois*, her husband Louis Prud'homme and their three sons Pierre, Jean Baptiste and Francois-Xavier; Pierre's brother, Jean-Baptiste and my cousin Jean Valiquet, who first introduced me to Pierre, for which I am most grateful. I'll never be able to remember all their names.

Now it's time to sit down and eat and drink. It was very warm in the church, and I know everyone is very thirsty. We have a large supply of chilled tea, wine and spirits and all the food one could desire. There are toasts to us all around. Pierre and I drink from a special two handled cup called a coupe de marriage which symbolizes our unity as man and wife. Lambert and Élizabeth do the same with theirs.

When all of us are sufficiently stuffed with the delicious food, the musicians strike up the band and the dancing begins. The four of us newlyweds start it off with our first dances. Then the family all take a turn with each of us. Soon the entire church yard is one kaleidoscopic swirl. If there is one thing that characterizes us as a people, it is our complete lack of inhibition. We love to sing and dance until we drop.

I've learned that here in the New World we are egalitarian. All the pretense between the classes and the prohibitions between levels of society, which exist back in France, have been abandoned in favor of a new system in which we are all equal. All of our varied work and talents are essential for our success as a colony. How can we not succeed!

The musicians decide they need a break, and we certainly need to rest awhile. It's a good time to dive into our scrumptious desserts of sweet pies and sucre la crème. I certainly never ate this well back in France. No one starves here in Ville-Marie!

All that maple sugar fortifies us for another round of dancing and then more dancing. I'm very glad I wore comfortable shoes under all my petticoats. Has this been the most fabulous wedding ever in New France, or am I a bit prejudiced? It's been so much fun and I think everyone has had a very good time. The bells in the church tower have been chiming the hours as they pass; twelve, one, two, three, four, five, six and now seven. Dusk is coming on and we will have to call it a day, or the mosquitoes will begin to feast on us. Everyone is getting tired and the time has come to say goodnight and thank you to all our guests. I hate to see it end, but all good things must, I know. I'll never forget this amazing day!

It's time for Pierre and me to head for his house. No, make that "our" home. I'm sure I'll soon get used to that notion. We say a quick goodbye to everybody, and head down the road to begin our new life together. We are both so very happy. As we approach the front door and Pierre opens it, he sweeps me up in his arms and carries me over the threshold. It is a few short steps to his large plump featherbed. Oh how I adore this man of mine! He decides it is time to fall to our knees and pray for God's blessing on our marriage and offer our thanks to Him for each other. Absolutely, I should have thought of it! What happens next shall remain ours alone. Bon nuit nos amis!

*Women kept their maiden names when they married.

# CHAPTER 12    HAPPINESS IS...

As our first morning together dawns, I decide to let Pierre sleep. I contemplate how I now enter the rest of my life as an adult. From now on it's no longer I and me, it's we and us. Mine has transformed into ours. I was an only child and hate to admit I was spoiled as much as was possible in our circumstances. It will actually be a pleasure to reform myself. I'm ready to blossom into the wife Pierre deserves, and a loving mother to our babies. I know there are no limits to how many children it is possible to love. Our love should stretch to envelop the whole world, for this is how God loves us. Pierre and I want to have as many children as possible. Since I've married at fourteen, I figure we can form a full farm crew.

As I rise and am able to survey my surroundings, I see that Pierre did a good job of sprucing up our home in anticipation of my arrival. Of course there may be a few touches I'd like to add. As I take a tour of our abode, I see we have a very large room that serves many functions. The focal point is an immense walk-in stone fireplace where I will cook our meals. At least I've had a head start in this department. I've been cooking for my father since shortly after my mother died. There is a nice large sturdy kitchen table and chairs with woven rush seats that can accommodate at least eight. This is situated at a comfortable distance from the fire so I can work on it easily. On the other side of the room there are a few comfortable chairs including a rocker, which is essential for a mother, and a small writing desk beneath a window. Our bedroom is private and the only other room on this level.

Upstairs is a very large open loft where all our children will sleep. I can hear their little voices now, giggling when they should be settling down, saying their prayers and going to sleep. There are two dormers up there with windows poking out of the roof on the front of our wooden home. Almost all the houses here are built of wood. I wish we had a few more windows to let in a little more light and fresh air on the first floor. We are situated facing the water. I realize that I'll be very happy we don't, when the frigid winter sets in especially because the St. Lawrence River freezes over. The wind over the ice can be biting. This will be my second winter here in Ville-Marie, so I know.

Most of our land is behind our house. There is a barn and chicken coop. There are separate pens for the pigs, a cow and two horses. Pierre has a very large garden he has been harvesting to put up for the winter. Since I was raised as a "town girl", I'll need to be schooled in food preservation. I guess I need to learn everything about farming in general. Nothing compares with learning by actually doing. If the bountiful harvest this year is any indication, we are situated on very fertile land. Thank you, Lord! Oh good, there is an enormous supply of firewood harvested from the surrounding woods. That must have taken him months to cut down, gather and split. I'm glad it isn't located too far from the back door.

My sweet husband interrupted my reverie with a kiss on the back of my neck. He scoops me up once again and carries me over the threshold of the back door this time. I see that life with Pierre will never be dull!

# CHAPTER 13  HIS DIABOLICAL PRESENCE CONFIRMED

After a few more days of blissful honeymooning, which we wished would never end, Pierre feels he better get back to his job at Fort Ville-Marie. I certainly understand. This is one reason I love him. He is so dependable. I can always count on him to do what he said he would.

I plan on spending the day gathering wild berries from the forest and fields to dry, with his sister Roberte. I need to get on with my education in food preservation. There is the slightest warning in the morning breeze signaling the end of summer. Pierre and I milked the cow, fed the chickens, and gathered their eggs, fed the pigs and horses before dawn. I guess I'm fortunate to be a morning person and to have married one. This will come in handy when the baby is born. I've never known a baby to sleep in late.

We then share a hearty breakfast of sausage, eggs, bread and tea. I pack him a dinner and snack to take to work. Then we part after a lingering kiss and hug. I watch him walk out the back door carrying his dinner basket and loaded musket which rarely leaves his side.

He passes his sister Roberte as she arrives laden down with berry buckets and the musket he made especially for her. I think there must be target practice in my near future. I'm not really looking forward to that aspect of life in the hinterlands.

I really like Roberte. She has been married to Louis Prud'homme for seven years. She is thirty-six years old and they have three young sons, so she will be a great help to me traversing the perils of life as a farmer and mother in Ville-Marie. She is happy to have a sister-in-law finally, since she only has two much younger brothers.

She turns down my offer of a cup of tea. So we set off together buckets and musket in tow. As we are walking and chatting about our fantastic wedding, she suddenly gets very quiet. I turn to her and ask what's wrong. She tears up, puts down the buckets and grasps my hand. She saw Corporal René Besnard dit Bourjoly in the church sneaking out the side door as we were beginning to exit! Oh my God! This is what I've dismissed from my mind with my usual optimistic outlook. She hadn't had the heart to let us know sooner than now. She has been mulling this over and over, and after consulting with her mother, they agreed we had to be made aware of his diabolical presence.

I have to sit down for a bit and collect myself. How will I ever tell Pierre? What will he do to René? Maybe he'll have faith that his Miserere antidote will work and we have absolutely nothing to worry about. He is bound to know something is very wrong with me, so I can't hide it from him. I don't want to begin our marriage with mistrust between us. Roberte agrees

34

that he has to be told. It's very possible someone else has informed him by now and he won't want to tell me.

Oh well, let's try to have a good day in spite of it all. It's a lovely day for berry picking. The fall blueberries and blackberries are nice and plump. Any raspberries I find, I just may eat along the way. I think they must be the food of the angels. Roberte doesn't disagree. She plans on gathering and gobbling them right behind me. No, on second thought we have to bring some to our families, especially Pierre, who will require something very special after I break the terrible news. I am beyond angry with René. How could he be so vengeful? He claims to love me, and this is what he wishes me! It's unbelievable. Talk about a sore loser!

It's time to turn around and head for home. At least our search has been very fruitful (pun intended). All of our buckets are full to the brim. We didn't need to stop for dinner because we'd found so many raspberries begging to be picked.

Pierre will be home soon and how I dread telling him. I've been pacing back and forth for close to an hour trying to find the words to break it to him gently.

He is coming up the stepping stones out front. I put on my biggest smile and hope he can't read the rest of my face. Pierre's face seems to be mirroring mine. I'm shocked to hear that everyone knows at the fort. Apparently René got very inebriated last night and told his story of cursing both of us with infertility to anyone who'd listen. He claims he was able to secretly knot a cord three times that he carried in his pocket. He is so very proud of himself. We decide that we just can't let him win. We must try to relax, let nature take its course and above all, try not to worry about it. Just put it out of our minds. Pierre had to admit though, that he had a very tough time refraining from beating him to a pulp.

# CHAPTER 14   ISLAND LIFE

Our tiny but growing village of Ville-Marie is located on the coast of the Ile de Montréal. There is a mountain in the middle of our island that Jacques Cartier climbed on October 3, 1535. He named it Mont Royal. The island is surrounded by two beautiful rivers: the Rivière des Prairies and the Saint Lawrence. Samuel de Champlain called our island Montréal on a map dated 1621 and the name has stuck. The various tribes of Indians have different names for the island and village, all very difficult to pronounce: Hochelaga, Tiohtia:ke, Tiohtia:ke Tsi, Ka-we-no-te and Moniang. And I thought French was a difficult language!

Today for our second month anniversary Pierre presented me with my very own handcrafted musket he made just for me and engraved my name on its hickory wood stock. Since I'm quite petite, it's not very easy for me to shoot one, let alone hit the target. I hope I will never be required to use it. I guess if I was ever faced with a life or death situation, my adrenaline would surge and overcome my handicaps. Just the threat of me behind a musket would make a few people think twice about menacing me. Who knows, I might get lucky and inflict some real damage.

Needless to say I thanked him with the most enthusiastic response I could muster. It's not the most romantic gift, but romance is not his strong suit. The fact that he wants to keep me around could be construed by some as very romantic!

In this remote village, with the threat of Iroquois ambushes still possible, despite our treaty with them, self-defense is always in the back of our minds. Most members of our village shed countless tears at the funeral of our dear friend and Notary Jean-de-Sainte-Père. He was our first town clerk (greffier) and also our first Notary Public. He just drew up our marriage contract in May. We also grieve for Nicholas Godi and Jacques Noel, who were also killed with him by the Iroquois on October 25, 1657. I hope never again to see such a tragic day.

Recently my cousin Jean Valiquet was subject to a vicious beating by, of all people, his next door neighbor, Jacques de la Porte dit Sainte-Georges. He was attacked right on his own doorstep. I was very concerned about him because he was very nearly killed. He remained under the surgeon Etienne Bouchard's care for twelve days. The town officials forced Jacques to pay the doctor for treating, lodging and feeding him during that two week period. I certainly hope he's learned his lesson. I think he got off much too easy. I don't envy Nicole. She married him only two months ago. She has to try and tame him somehow. I wish her luck.

This makes me very grateful for my sweetheart, who I know would never hurt anyone. I can't imagine the circumstances that would provoke him to violence.

After all, René remains unscathed, despite every provocation.

One thing about muskets really frightens me. They must always be kept loaded because it takes too long to load them for effective self-defense. You would be shot dead by the time you got the powder, lead ball and wad loaded into the barrel. I pray that no one I know and love is accidentally shot with one.

I think I'm taking well to life as a farmer's wife. I hope Pierre would agree. I do know I'm giving it my all. I soon realized there were two vital things missing from our living room. I needed to purchase a spinning wheel and loom. Now I'm learning how to operate them. It turns out we own a dozen sheep. I hadn't noticed them grazing in the field, on my first tour of the farm. They'll provide the wool which I'll shear once I learn how. Then I'll make blankets and fabric on the loom and knit sweaters, hats, mittens etc. during the long winter months. I like to keep busy.

I'm also learning how to ride a horse, and I haven't fallen off yet! Of course I prudently chose the smaller and more docile one named Grace. We took to each other right away. She is a beautiful brown Bay with a diamond shaped patch on her wise face. I say wise because I'm sure she understands everything I confide in her. She's a very good listener.

Pierre's horse is a splendid black stallion named Lightning, for obvious reasons. Lightning can really move. Come to think of it, Grace is the only horse for me! Both of them have given us very enjoyable hours of riding and surveying our domain made more glorious by Our Lord's amazing fall leaf display. Grace and Lightning peaceably graze together without the slightest friction. I do love horses and always have. Not in my wildest dreams did I ever expect to have one of my very own. I feel that God got it all just right when he created the horse.

I think we'd all agree that another of God's masterpieces is the cow. What would life and French cooking be without the milk, cream, cheese and especially butter she gladly gives to us? Our poor cow had no name.

Pierre, inexplicably, had never gotten around to naming the sweet creature with the big soulful eyes. So I thought long and hard about what we should call her. I hoped to dignify her existence and show her how much we truly appreciate her vital contribution to our family. So I gave her the much revered name of Collette. Collette was a much loved fifteenth century French nun who gave everything she owned to the poor, and founded the order of the Poor Clares. I just know that someday she will be canonized a Saint. So it is especially fitting that we give her this name for she gives us her all, everyday twice a day, at 5am and 5pm.

# CHAPTER 15   OUR FIRST CHRISTMASTIDE

As we approach the Christmas season with two feet of twinkling snow blanketing the village, all of us ladies are busily preparing for the coming feast days. I've been putting the spinning wheel, loom and knitting needles through their paces as I make gifts for every member of the family and Pierre of course.

All of this bustle must not distract us from our preparation for our Lord's coming at the close of Advent. This is a four week time of penance and fasting in our church tradition, a period of anticipation and spiritual reflection for the coming of the Christ Child on December 25th and His eventual Second Coming "at a time only the Father knows".

The children of the village have a difficult time with these concepts and wait in joyful dreaming about the sweets and gifts they will receive on Christmas Eve and New Years' Day. Keeping all this a secret must be a challenge for their parents.

Today is our fourth month anniversary and I'm still without child. That's the only gift I'll ever need or want. How I envy all the expectant moms and there are many in our little town. I so want to join in on their gleeful conversations and preparations. Everyone knows all about the position we are in, so they get very quiet when I'm around. It's becoming more awkward every day. I've told them not to worry about me. I'll join their throng when the time is right.

They know of the perils they and their babies face but it doesn't seem to worry them. The child mortality rate in the first few months of life is great. I've noticed that the babies born in the warmer months seem to stand a better chance of surviving. I hope God's timing will give me a summertime baby.

It's difficult to keep warm for us adults also. Many of us succumb in winter, especially our senior members. A place near the fire is cherished. Another reason to be grateful I was born a woman, with all the cooking I must do I've become a fireplace dweller.

Our homes are built much closer together than you'd expect for farmland. The land is divided into long rectangles with our land stretching far behind the houses. This makes us able to socialize easily and protect each other from attack. We can run next door for refuge or simply to enjoy a cup of tea and cookies. We all love to play cards and board games. This is a very popular pastime all year long. Of course we all usually rise early with the rooster and retire early, just after dark when our work is done, with winter being the only exception because the sun sets then at four o'clock. The benefit for us farmers in the winter is that our workload is lessened greatly. The harvest is in, preserved and put up in crocks or in the root cellars. The ground is frozen solid so I have this abiding fear of falling on the ice and breaking a bone.

Presently Mom, Roberte and I are planning the menu for the Reveillon feast on Christmas after the Christmas Eve Mass. The word reveil means wakening. I think this is the reason it is called the wakening: the children are put to bed at the normal time and then awakened to accompany their parents to Midnight Mass in hopes that they will be able to stay awake long enough to enjoy the beautiful Christmas carols at Mass and the feast following. They also open their stockings filled with sweets and small gifts.

I was delighted to learn that we brought this tradition with us from France when we immigrated to the New World. We will all share the cooking and clean up. We will stage it at Pierre's parents' home this year. We've decided to rotate our homes so that no one has to bear the load every year. This feast breaks our Advent fast and is a glorious way to celebrate the Baby Jesus, the light of the world Who dispels the darkness and comes to save us.

Every family has a handmade crèche with little carved figures of the nativity scene. As a child I remember placing a bit of straw in the empty manger for every good deed I did through Advent. Then I got to place Him, the tiny Christ Child figurine in his overflowing manger after Christmas Eve Mass. How much I loved this honor. This year Roberte's son Francois-Xavier will do this and treasure the memory always, as I do.

The menu can be as elaborate as we desire. Back in France I understood the nobility would have a thirteen course feast, one for Jesus and the twelve apostles. The servants had to wash all the dishes and try to keep up with the flow between courses behind the scenes. That's ridiculous and probably has killed more than one noble or servant in the eating or the doing.

We colonists have scaled this down to a more reasonable festive meal. We'll have Tortiere, which is traditional. This special meat pie is made with ground pork, potatoes and four specific spices are required: cinnamon, cloves, allspice and nutmeg. Everyone has their favorite family recipe handed down for Tortiere, but all are encased in a rich buttery flaky pastry. We will also serve baked beans, meat stew, pea soup, pickled beets, and various garnishes. We top this off for dessert with sugar pie and the essential Buche de Noel, a scrumptious cake that resembles the Birch wood log which is kept burning in the fireplace all night long–our Yule log.

We all decorate our homes for the twelve days of Christmas. This is the time between Christmas Eve at midnight and the feast of the Epiphany on January sixth. The Epiphany or Three King's Day commemorates the Magi coming to find and worship Jesus by following the Star of Bethlehem, bearing gold, frankincense and myrrh. We place fragrant fresh pine or fir boughs on the mantelpiece and table tops accented with pine cones and acorns and light as many candles as is possible to provide a cheery atmosphere. This also is emblematic of Christ's coming as the Light of the World. I've always thought it fitting that we celebrate His arrival at the darkest time in the calendar year.

New Years' Day is a special day for the children who are allowed to open their larger gifts then. Of course we have another special meal to welcome in the Vielle du Jour de L'an (New Years' Day) I will host the meal this year 1658 for the first time as an official member of Pierre's family. Everyone knows the good fortune we pray for this year. May our dear Lord grant us our fondest wish if it be His will.

# CHAPTER 16    SPRINGTIME–SEASON OF HOPE

As the St. Lawrence thaws with a resounding crack, we put up our raquettes (snowshoes) for the season. The maple sap has been harvested from the trees. How grateful we are to that first Indian tribesman who accidentally discovered this heavenly liquid when he hit that sugar maple tree with his hatchet. Our long dreary, but active winter is exiting with barely a whimper.

My playful puppy Brigitte has grown so large in the past three months. Pierre surprised me with her for my birthday on January twenty-second. She is going to be a very large, eighty-five pound dog when fully grown because she is a Le Chien de Montagne des Pyrénées. The breed is native to the French Pyrénées Mountains, and is renowned for their ability to fiercely guard both their flocks of sheep as well as their families. Her astoundingly thick all white coat protected her from the cold winter winds, yet she seems as delighted as we are to see the first green grass sprigs emerge through the snow cover. She has spent hours conscientiously investigating what her sheep have been dining on today.

It is eight months since our wedding day, so Pierre and I have decided to consult with Father Pijart about our ongoing predicament. He couldn't be more sympathetic when he told us that the Church's policy with past witchcraft cases back in France was that the couple should first pray about it. Of course he knows we have more than fulfilled this requirement. Then we should confess our sins and receive Holy Communion. Sometimes the couple may require the rite of exorcism but thankfully since he sees no evidence of demonic possession in us that process will not be necessary. The next step is arranging for another Nuptial Blessing by our Bishop Francois de Laval up in Québec. We agree that we are anxious to do whatever is necessary as soon as feasible. He warned us not to try and contact René Besnard to reverse the spell. This would be a further work of the devil. Since that remedy had never even occurred to us, we vowed that neither of us would ever resort to adding evil upon evil in this manner. Father will send a letter to the Bishop today to explain our situation, and tell him that we are requesting a second Nuptial Blessing upon our marriage.

The St. Lawrence River is now passable and mail can move by boat on the river to Québec more easily now. We promised to be available whenever the Bishop wishes to see us. I suggest we should wait to make the Nuptial Blessing coincide with our first anniversary on August twelfth. My friend Catherine in Québec is pregnant with her second child and is due around the end of May. This should give her time to recover. This way the Bishop will have plenty of advance notice. Then we parted from our dear Father on that hopeful note.

I'm so very happy at the prospect of returning to Québec and seeing where Catherine and her husband

Charles live with their sweet little one, Anne. We'll also get to see their new addition to the family. I'm sure Catherine will want us to stay with them. Pierre used to live in Québec for a short time as a young boy when his family first arrived from France.

Pierre is thrilled that we are able to have our marriage blessed again, by the Bishop no less, in a completely different city and church minus René. If this doesn't wash us clean of the abhorrent hex, he doesn't know what will. It's absolutely essential that we keep this trip a secret from everyone except Pierre's parents. René must never find out our plans.

The next three months passed swiftly giving neither of us time to dwell on our troubles. The pace of farm life accelerates in the sweet warm months of summer. I think it has now become my favorite season of the year, despite the sweltering heat I must endure when cooking in the fireplace.

We're both looking forward to our anniversary trip up the river to Québec. It will be a welcome respite from both the fort and our farm duties. We've hired a young family friend to fill in for us, feeding all the animals and milking Collette.

We just heard that Catherine and their little Catherine born June first are both thriving and can't wait to see us. I'll never be able to catch up with Catherine's baby production! How wonderful that they are so blessed by God's best gifts!

We decided to keep this next Nuptial Blessing a very toned down affair. There will be only Bishop de Laval presiding with Catherine, Charles and their two babies present to witness the event.

Before we board the boat for the short trip north, we thank God for His Providence over our first year together and plead for His help in rectifying René's wrong upon us. It is a crystal clear day as we sail upon azure blue water. I'm inspired to beseech Our Lady as we drift along the Madonna blue river. She must understand my longing to give birth to our first child. My offering of my bridal bouquet to her a year ago comes to mind as I allow hot tears to flow. There is no point in trying to hold them back, no point at all. Pierre notices and squeezes my hand as his eyes read my mind and search my heart.

Charles meets us at the pier with kisses and a big bear hug for me and jovial handshake and a kiss on both cheeks for Pierre which we warmly return. This is customary both in France and New France. It's a short stroll up to their home. Charles is a bourgeois so his surname is Gauthier, Sieur de Boisverdun. He was born in Paris in 1630 and is eight years older than Catherine. He looks the picture of a proud and happy husband and father as he throws open the front door of his home and gleefully announces "They're here!" What a wonderful warm feeling embraces this family and home, so much so that our grey mood turns upside down in a flash. Tomorrow we meet our Bishop accompanied by such a precious family who are fairly brimming over with joy. Yes, I'm so glad Bishop de Laval is stationed in Québec so that we are able to change our surroundings for a time.

The next day starts at six o'clock with the hungry cries of two little ones. I'm happy to feed Anne her breakfast while her mom breastfeeds Catherine in the rocker under the window. What a poignant vignette they make bathed in the pink light of dawn breaking over the horizon. Next we prepare a hearty breakfast of ham and eggs, toast and fresh butter for the four of us.

After dressing ourselves and the babies in their darling tiny clothes, we are all off to the Church nearby for a new yet familiar experience, private morning Mass climaxing with our special Nuptial Blessing. We do not renew our vows but the cherished memories of last years' promises to each other come surging back for both of us as Pierre reaches for my hand.

We thank Bishop de Laval for his kindness and special blessing. He clasps his hands around mine and his blue eyes search mine before I have a chance to bow down and kiss his ring. We'd never met until today yet I feel he is able to discern the depth of my spirit. He is a true shepherd of souls, a worthy reflection of Jesus, chosen by Him for this difficult post, this fledgling colony.

We gather up the children and head for their home feeling much heartened by our reception of Jesus from the Bishop and his special blessing upon us from above.

Dinner was all ready and waiting for us in the cook pot we left simmering over the fire. Catherine is an excellent cook, having been trained by her mom from a young age. As we mop up the last bit of gravy from our bowls, Charles gingerly introduces the topic of a second plan that he has been mulling over since he first heard we were coming. He, as a seigneur and member of Québec's seigneurial tribunal, knows Mathurin Langevin, Sieur de la Croix. He is the cousin of my cousin Jean Valiquet, but no relation of mine except being a good friend to both of us who attended our wedding. Charles is sure that Mathurin would agree with him that witchcraft is an abomination better left in France. The court in Montréal should try René Besnard dit Bourjoly for sorcery. This trial would serve as a warning to deter all future incidents of this evil. This would be the first trial for witchcraft in New France. If found guilty, which seems very likely since there are so many witnesses, the punishment is severe, burning at the stake is even a possibility. Pierre is immediately receptive to the whole idea, while I'm sitting there dumbfounded.

Catherine sits staring incredulously at her husband for a long while and then turns to me. We are both thinking the same thought, I believe. Are these the same sweet gentle men we married such a short time ago? Men really are a different species entirely. We both have vowed obedience to them, so they do have the last say about something so crucial. Catherine and I do not venture an opinion except to excuse ourselves to go and put the babies down for their naps.

Then we step outside and head for the bench under a sprawling oak tree to begin to decipher what in the world they are thinking. We both understand the deterrent value of prosecuting René, but really can't abide the ghastly notion of him burning at the stake. Catherine accidentally saw this punishment carried out as a little girl back in France and was traumatized. The idea of such a barbaric act here in our new colony! Maybe this New World isn't as different as we hoped.

## CHAPTER 17   JUSTICE IS SERVED

After just a few days respite in Québec City we head for home relaxed, refreshed and renewed with hope in our hearts that the second blessing will have the desired effect. We have agreed to wait a few more months to see if I conceive before launching further action against René.

We are greeted by the surprising news that my cousin Jean has chosen a mate, or maybe she chose him, from this year's crop of twenty-seven marriageable girls who arrived this summer from all over France. A total of eight ships came in carrying fourteen girls bound for Montreal, eleven for Québec City and two for Trois-Rivières. This is the first year our total has exceeded Québec City.

His choice, Renée Loppé, decided to make the voyage after having lost both parents by the age of thirteen, so that makes Jean her senior by thirteen years. They plan to sign their marriage contract and marry one month from now. We are so very happy for them, although I hope they are not rushing a little too fast into this serious commitment. I do know how very lonely Jean has been, and I'm sure Renée misses the love and comfort of family as I did.

These continue to be treacherous times for our little colony. The Iroquois seem to have stepped up their ongoing war on us. Governor de Maisonneuve has decided to begin construction of our town's first water well. Jacques Archambault is in charge of the project inside the walls of Fort Ville-Marie. I pray he is successful and that this is the first of many wells all over town that would revolutionize and simplify our lives.

Now it's time for me to get back to work on our farm harvesting and preserving the crops for the coming winter. All of our animals seemed very relieved to see me, especially Brigitte, who nearly knocked me down expressing her joy. She followed me around the rest of the day to insure I didn't disappear. This was out of character for her since she is usually obsessed with the surveillance of her flock and the rest of our creatures. I think she considers me her lost sheep that she will never allow out of her sight again. I'm anxious to see her reaction to Pierre's return this evening.

She didn't have a very long wait to spot him sprinting up to where I stood smiling at the back door. Then she witnessed Pierre gather me up in his arms and carry his bride around the house and over the threshold once more, this time accompanied by Brigitte's bewildered barking. I could tell by the pace of his jaunt that the stew for supper would have to simmer a while longer in the fireplace.

While our Dear Lord begins to paint the sugar maple trees their gorgeous range of vibrant shades of reds, oranges and yellows, all on single tree, I marvel at His abiding love for His creatures on this plane. He provides this burst of every color imaginable every year for a short time, like a grand finale while they exit the stage and rest for the winter. Golden autumn is a spectacular but fleeting glimpse of what His heaven must look like, eternal life with Him in a world saturated in pure color, awash in His pure love. He has promised we will have no more worries, no more strife, no more tears in His Paradise restored.

As the last leaf falls to the earth, our watching and waiting period has expired. I really don't feel that prosecuting René will help our situation but Pierre feels we need to be released from this land of limbo by grasping the reins and commencing action. I reluctantly agree to his wishes, although I don't look forward to the trial of the culprit that has wreaked havoc on our lives.

Corporal René Besnard dit Bourjoly is ordered to appear before the Seigneurial Court of Montréal at nine o'clock on November second to answer charges of sorcery against the injured couple Pierre Gadois and Marie Pontonnier. Several other citizens are joining our complaint against him.

That morning dawned with a profound chill in the air. Louis d'Ailleboust, Seigneur de Coulonge acting as chief magistrate called the Seigneurial Tribune Court to order. He read the charges of sorcery against René of attempting to render Pierre Gadois and Marie Pontonnier infertile. He asked Corporal Besnard how he pleaded against these charges. He pleads innocent. Francoise Bénard, twenty eight years old, was sworn in and testified that Besnard told her he knew of a spell which would render a couple sterile for a period of seventeen years if the incantation was said over a string that he would tie in a knot three times in the presence of this couple at their marriage ceremony. Jeanne Godard, twenty years old, who had just arrived in Montréal this past summer also testified that he bragged to her of this spell that he was able to accomplish in their presence.

I asked to testify so that I could relate the obscene proposal that he presented to me. He had the unmitigated gall to say that he would reverse the spell if I agreed to have sexual relations with him. I returned to my seat blushing red all over from total embarrassment as would any lady in that situation. Several others testified because he certainly had not kept it a secret from anyone before or after our wedding ceremony, a fact that I could never comprehend.

René had his opportunity to refute these charges. Confronted with testimony that he boasted of "knowing how to tie the knot, and who tied it for her husband" he claimed that he was speaking of lacing a corset. Besnard admitted speaking with Jeanne, but claimed not to remember what the conversation was about. He denied using sorcery on the couple, but alleged that it was Marie who had promised him the fullest intimacies if he would acknowledge the deed and break the spell. He claimed that it was she who suggested the antidote, not the other way around as I had testified. He had been caught in his own web of lies by that statement. He was acknowledging that he had indeed done the act of which he is accused.

He further testified that he was only joking if he spoke about witchcraft in an effort to scare Pierre. At this point in the proceedings it was obvious that he was terrified that he had not convinced them of his innocence and he would be convicted and burned alive at the stake for his sorcery. This is the usual punishment meted out in France for this offense.

Instead he was found guilty and ordered imprisoned for an indefinite period of time, to be decided later, and upon release, exiled from Montréal forever. We had just witnessed the first witchcraft trial in New France and hopefully the last.

I was relieved that he wouldn't be burnt at the stake. Pierre was thrilled that he would never have to lay eyes on him again at the fort or anywhere in Ville-Marie.

We returned to our farm somehow revived by the guilty verdict, as if some great black cloud which had hung above us for the past year and a half had suddenly dissolved and we were now free to pursue our lives without this curse following our every move. This may be a foolish reaction but we will revel in the feeling while it lasts. Pierre's mood was ebullient, so we got right to starting the family we both want so very dearly.

As Pierre and I wait, hope and pray for a baby, I thought I'd turn the spotlight on my neighbors for a welcome change.

I was delighted when my cousin Jean found Renée Loppé to marry and be the mother of his children. His five year recruitment contract with the Grande Recrue of 1653 would have expired in November and he could have elected to leave Ville-Marie and return to France without cost to him, as some men are doing this fall. We don't need further shrinkage in our colony.

Here is a typical contract for two recruits that Governor de Maisoneuve submitted to two men in my hometown of La Flèche Anjou, France five years ago:

## Enlistment Contract of Urbain Jette and Rene Maillet

The thirtieth day of March one thousand six hundred fifty-three after noon, before us, Pierre de La Fousse, royal notary and record keeper at La Flèche and resident thereof, were present, settled and submitted squire Paul de Chomedy, Sieur de La Dauversiere, procurator of the Company of Associates for the Conversion of the Savages of New France on the said Isle of Montreal, the said Sieur de Maisonneuve residing at the said Fort of Ville-Marie on the said isle and the said Sieur de La Dauversiere residing at the said La Flèche on one side; and Urbain

Jetté, longsawyer and mason residing in the Faubourg
Saint-Jacques of the said La Flèche and René Maillet,
cooper from Sainte Colombe, both present, have made
and granted what follows: That is the said Jetté and
Maillet have promised and obligated themselves to
serve on the said Isle of Montréal in their respective
trades and in other tasks that may be asked of them
for which they may be found capable for the period of
five whole and consecutive years to begin from the day
that they shall arrive at the said isle under the
command of the said Sieur de Maisonneuve, to which
end they have promised and obligated themselves in
body and goods to make their way to the dwelling of
Master Charles Lecoq, Sieur de La Bassonniere in the
town of Nantes on the last day of April to embark with
the said Sieur de Maisonneuve for the said land, for
which the said Sieurs de Maisonneuve and De La
Dauversiere in their said names have promised to
feed, lodge and shelter them during the voyage as well
as during the said term of their service and at the end
of which to conduct them back to France at their cost
and expense without cost to the said Jetté and Maillet
and to furnish them with all the tools necessary for the
tasks in which they shall be employed, in addition to
paying the sum of ninety livres to each of the said
Jetté and Maillet each year in wages, payable to each
of them at the end of each of the said five years, except
that for the first year they shall be advanced what
shall be necessary to equip them. That which is above
has been stipulated and agreed to by the parties. And
for this keeping and obliging and renouncing, etc.
Done at the said La Flèche in the presence of René

Maillet, practician and Francois Hardy, also a practician residing at the said La Flèche, witnesses, and the said Maillet and Jetté declared not to know how to sign their names.
(Signed) Paul de Chomedey, Le Royer de la Dauversiere, Hardy, De La Fousse, notary

Of the one hundred fifty men that originally signed similar contracts, one hundred·three showed up to board the sailing ship. Of that Grand Recrue contingent, eight died on the transatlantic voyage, twenty·four have since been killed by the Iroquois and five in accidents. The remaining sixty·seven survivors are absolutely essential to our colony's survival. Of course Renée is more thrilled than I that she found and married Jean before he had a chance to slip away. Renée, thirteen years old is two years younger than I am, so I've decided with her permission to take her under my wing and help her learn the ropes of life in our hinterlands. At last I've found the younger sister I've always wanted.

It's a frozen winter wonderland again this year which is a bit of a shock to her, as it was to all of us transplants when we first arrived. How we wish warm beaver fur hats were as popular with us colonists as they are in Europe. We can't send them enough beaver pelts. I heard that every year in the 1600s we've shipped 20,000 beaver pelts to France alone.

Here in Montréal we are fortunate to be a strategic location for the canoes full of pelts to be off loaded onto ships bound for the homeland. In the winter some pelts are loaded onto dog or horse drawn sleds that skim the ice on the frozen St. Lawrence River to Ville-Marie.

These pelts are acquired by coureur des bois (runners in the woods) who are independent entrepreneurs that travel far into the woods to trade imported European items with friendly Indians. Things like hatchets, knives and cook pots are willingly exchanged for beaver pelts that the Indians have trapped and prepared. These are a very valuable export for us and the Indians are delighted to get the items they need very much. What these men are doing is actually illegal, because King Louis XIV has established a royal trade monopoly in the furs. Many of the coureur des bois are killed when venturing west and north into hostile Iroquois territory.

The Algonquin people became allies of the French in the fur trade while the Iroquois became allies of the British. The friendly Huron were virtually wiped out by smallpox in the 1630s that we Europeans unwittingly brought them. The Iroquois to the south pounced on this opportunity to eliminate their hated enemy, the once powerful Huron nation north of the St. Lawrence River and the Great Lakes. This was accomplished in 1648. Jesuit Father Jean de Brebeuf was martyred during the Iroquois raid on the remaining Huron at Saint-Ignace on March 16, 1649. The few remaining Huron, originally 30,000 strong were dispersed and ceased to be a nation.

The call of the wilderness still attracts a certain intrepid breed of French explorer/fur trader despite all the possible perils that can befall them. The pursuit of pelts entails long arduous travel with frequent stops to carry their heavily laden birch bark canoes over land many times to reach passable water. They eventually cover hundreds of miles to acquire the large monetary reward that awaits the lucky surviving coureur des bois.

There was a remarkably resilient thirty-three year old female passenger travelling with the men of the Grande Recrue by the name of Marguerite Bourgeoys. In the intervening five years she has wrought miracles for our colony. She was chosen by the sister of Governor Maisonneuve who happened to be the director of the cloistered convent of the Congregation of Notre Dame in Troyes, Champagne, France. The Governor was over there visiting when he asked if she knew anyone who would like to take on the assignment of teaching the children of the settlers and of Amerindian people in Ville-Marie. Marguerite was her choice among several willing candidates.

Marguerite had never wanted to join the cloister because of her overwhelming desire to help the poor. She felt the cloistered life was not the mission that our Lord had in mind for her in this world. Instead she became an extern, took a vow of chastity and pledged herself to a life that mirrored the Virgin Mary as much as possible helping her fellow man.

We are so fortunate that she agreed to accompany the Governor and his one hundred-three recruits to Ville-Marie. Everyone knows and reveres her here, although at first there were very few children for her to teach because of our very high mortality rate. Her fervent goal of teaching took a step closer to reality when this past January twenty-second Governor Maisonneuve gave her an abandoned converted stable to live in and begin in earnest her school.

She soon left for France with Jeanne Mance, who could find care for her broken arm that hadn't healed properly, to go recruit more women to join her as teachers of our children, who thankfully have increased in number in the five years since she first arrived. My most cherished hope is that my children will have this brave and holy woman as their teacher.

# CHAPTER 19    SHATTERED DREAMS

It's the day after New Year's Day 1660, a time for introspection and resolutions. I confess that I can only see a long dark corridor ahead of me devoid of light at the end, and with every month that passes, another crushing disappointment bearing down upon us. We have been married for two years and four months and now the stress is opening cracks in the formerly strong foundation of our marriage.

We're facing another winter with more time to fill on our hands, all alone in our home that by now should resound with the delighted gurgles and giggles of our babies. How has it come to this Lord, and where do we go from here? I'm afraid there is no easy answer to this hopeless quagmire. I feel myself sinking into a quicksand that threatens to swallow me if I don't find a branch to cling to soon. I'm afraid that I am slipping into a deep depression which is a terrifying foreign territory for this normally gleeful girl.

Now that the two of us have gone through the motions of the holidays, I feel we must address the problem. I know the time has come to have that overdue talk with Pierre that we both have been deftly avoiding for months. We've been putting off the inevitable, when that never solves anything but just prolongs the agony. When I finally summon up the courage to speak to him, he blurts out that he will always love me even if I never give him children but he knows that I will never be content without them. I know in my heart and mind he is right.

We both agree that it is time to seek the advice of the dear priest who married us, Father Claude Pijart. I make an appointment to see him tomorrow afternoon for counseling. He has been expecting us for some time since he couldn't help but notice the strain on our faces as the months passed. He has been fervently praying as we have, that I would conceive and this visit would not be necessary.

A year and a half ago when we requested the second Nuptial Blessing on our marriage from Bishop Laval, the bishop informed him of the passage in the canon law of the church that pertains to our very unusual dilemma. It reads that after a waiting period of three years, the couple may mutually agree to annul the marriage "because of permanent infertility caused by an evil spell".

Since Pierre and I both feel that our marriage has been irrevocably destroyed by this atrocious evil curse, we decide that this is our only recourse. Father Pijart agrees to request this annulment for us from the bishop, to go into effect after our third anniversary. We return to our home in stunned silence. The next eight months will prove to be more difficult than either of us could possibly envision. We learn to live as brother and sister under the roof of the home that once held such promise.

We finally find the strength to break the news of our plans to his family. They were not aware of the possibility of an annulment on these grounds since our situation is so very rare. I feel they are almost as crushed as we are that this abomination has been done to us and left us with no other alternative if we wish to have a family. Their hearts are shattered as we depart their home in tears all around. There is nothing left to say.

I am losing so very much. This family I call mine will drift away from me ever so slowly but inexorably. No one, family members or friends can truly understand the ordeal that Corporal René Besnard dit Bourjoly unconscionably has put us through. How we rue the black day he entered our lives. I can't help but feel totally responsible, for back then I wanted to take my time making sure that Pierre was the right husband for me. If only I had chosen him immediately and run with him straight to the altar. No, I had to be cautious and allow René into our lives. This is all my fault and I will have to live with the realization of the grief I have caused Pierre for the rest of my life.

My adopted little sister Renée Loppé and my cousin Jean, the only real family I have left, have been my lifeline during these excruciatingly long months. They have offered to take me in for the last two months before our annulment becomes final on August thirtieth and for as long as I want to stay. I hate to intrude on the newlyweds but they insist that I must since they've noticed I'm losing weight from the stress and am suffering more than I'm willing to admit.

They are right of course and I agree to accept their kind offer of a port in the endless storm that has become my life. I hope I can be of assistance to Renée since she is due to deliver their first child in mid-September. I assure them that my stay will be brief, just until I can get my bearings. I have hope that God will lead me by the hand into the next phase of my life, as I tentatively proceed trying to take just one day at a time by one tiny step at a time.

Since Pierre still cares deeply about me he insists that I must do what is necessary for my physical and mental health. I am not to worry about the farm and the animals even though this is our busiest season. He will hire a farmhand or maybe two to look after the animals and help him bring in the harvest.

When I find my next situation and if it's practical, Pierre wants me to have Brigette because she was a birthday gift from him on my first birthday with him. In the meantime I should visit her whenever I'm able. I'm so grateful to him for that because I will sorely miss my faithful shepherd as well as my dear sweet horse and confidante Grace. I know that no one is indispensable so I'm sure this home and farm that I've poured all my love and strength into maintaining can go on without me. The question remains: Can I go on without it?

I return the next day with Renée to pack up my things while Pierre is at the fort. I cannot bear a tearful goodbye just now. There is no way to stop the tears from flowing as I'm loading my satchels. If he were here, I might not have the courage to walk out that door.

# CHAPTER 20   LET'S BEGIN AGAIN

The time has come to consult Marguerite
Bourgeoys, the most enlightened member of our
colony. If anyone can set my head on straight it's our
beloved teacher, surrogate mother, and living saint
who returned to us from France last September
twenty-ninth 1659. Governor Maisonneuve, Father
Souart and the entire colony were at the dock to greet
them. They arrived after a two month harrowing
voyage on what was once a wartime hospital ship, the
Sainte-Andre, which tragically was prophetic because
a "fievre maligne" soon broke out and eight passengers
succumbed to the plague at sea and more died after
they reached land.

Fortunately none of her recruits were stricken.
They were still a large group of forty-seven women and
sixty-two men. The females included thirteen married
women, nine young girls, three Sisters of Saint Joseph
who will serve at our hospital, the Hotel-Dieu de
Montreal, and their leader Jeanne Mance whose arm
was miraculously cured at the tomb of Abbe Olier, four
candidates for Marguerite's newly formed
Congregation Notre Dame who will become nuns and
schoolteachers for our children. She also accompanied
eighteen filles à marier destined for Québec and
Montréal. There were also two priests from Sainte-
Sulpice, Fathers Vignal and Lemaistre aboard the
ship. All these new arrivals in 1659 were sponsored by
the Societe Notre-Dame de Montreal, the order of

Sainte Sulpice, and the friends of the Hotel-Dieu de Montreal.

There are many changes as we struggle to survive and grow. Marguerite is also housing twelve of the filles à marier in her stable loft side by side on straw mattresses. The accommodations are primitive but the girls have the added advantage of her motherly wise counsel in courtship and marriage. Marguerite is also acting as matchmaker since she has come to know the girls on the voyage and their hopeful suitors so well.

I am sorely in need of her guidance also on my similar situation. I told her that my cousin Jean has informed me that there is another Pierre who I once had on my short list of favorites four years ago. Pierre Martin dit La Rivière of the Grande Recrue of 1653 has never married. He is a surgeon and interpreter for the militia and has confided to Jean that he still cares for me very much. I do remember him fondly and would like to find out if we can pick up where we left off.

My marriage annulment is now final since Bishop Francois de Laval made his first pastoral visit to Montréal and signed it last week on August thirtieth. I hope it is not improper to be thinking of another relationship so soon. She assured me that it is definitely fine and proper and Pierre Martin is a wonderful man of the finest character. She knows him very well having left France for the first time with the Grande Recrue seven years ago and travelled that long voyage with him and the other one hundred-two men. She sees us as a perfect match and knows that he would make an excellent father for our children.

Happy to receive her blessing and feeling much lighter in general, I give Jean permission to invite Pierre Martin for dinner as soon as possible. How heartening it is to have something to look forward to for a change! If Pierre is as willing as I've been told he is, I have no intention of dawdling this time.

I prepare a special Saturday meal for our reunion dinner for four. While it simmered, I fussed over my clothes and hair, deciding to let it fall down my back since Jean says all men love long hair. I'll add a few colorful ribbons to dress it up a bit. Now with that September crispness in the air I don't mind the extra weight of my thick mane. I decide to wear my midnight blue frock trimmed in white lace, flattering yet sedate.

My heart is beating faster in girlish anticipation which takes me by surprise. I have to admit to myself that I never quite forgot Pierre number two. I've wondered whether he was content as a bachelor or maybe his work kept him so busy he didn't have time to be lonely. I couldn't help but notice him sitting all alone in church, averting his eyes as I walked in arm in arm with Pierre.

I'm so glad he didn't ship back to France last fall when his contract expired for a lesser man might have. No, he has a sterling character which has always

71

attracted me and those big turquoise blue eyes which are most unusual in a French man, at once sparkling and gentle. Yes, I do admire his selflessness that steered him into his frustrating profession as a surgeon. We know so little about how the body and brain work and what to do to make it whole again.

My reverie is pleasantly interrupted when I hear his footsteps at the front door. I dash to fling the door open and our eyes meet. When he reaches for my hand to kiss it and before he has a chance, I pull him towards me for a kiss on both cheeks from me while on tiptoe and I receive a big hug from him in return. Yes, I think we can begin where we left off, despite the blush of shyness coloring his face I always found so endearing.

After Renée and Jean greet him and I introduce her to him, she insists that the three of us sit down and she will serve us dinner. She signals to me imperceptibly, by squeezing my hand, that she likes what she sees. Of course she is careful to point out to him that I have done all of the cooking for this meal because she is still a novice in the kitchen.

He always liked whatever I served him, and was so easy to please, having eaten army fare or whatever he kept in his sack while out on the trail. Home cooking is a very rare wonderful treat for all the recruits.

I can always be counted on to keep the dinner conversation moving and Renée is quite talkative also.

The men see a lot of each other at the fort so seem to welcome our chatter about anything else. The dinner is quite delicious and there are ample compliments from the men for which I express my appreciation.

Now that we have eaten our fill including dessert, Jean brings up the talk of the town which is the amazing battle of Long Sault that has saved our colony from slaughter at the hands of the Iroquois. We lost seventeen brave militia and our Algonquin and Huron allies lost forty-four of their brave warriors. The few surviving Huron lived to tell us the tale.

It was a grueling five-day battle in early May this past spring. Our militia found out that the Iroquois were amassing significant forces south of Montréal to eventually attack us. Our twenty-five year old garrison commander Adam Dollard des Ormeaux decided to take a few canoes and men, with the Governor's permission, down the Ottawa River. They loaded them with food, weapons and ammunition and set off, but soon encountered terrific resistance from the strong current just off our island. It took a week to reach their destination where they determined it was a good place for an ambush.

They decided to occupy an old Algonquin fort along the Ottawa River that was built of trees planted in a circle and then sawed off to their trunks. Forty Huron joined them along with their Chief Etienne Annahotaha. Commander Dollard decided to build a palisade around the fort as additional fortification but couldn't complete it before two-to three-hundred

Iroquois arrived and immediately assaulted our fort
and four of their warriors were killed. They decide to
build their own fort but first they requested a parley.

Dollard refused to speak to the Iroquois because
he didn't trust them. The Iroquois became so enraged
they decided to break up our unguarded canoes, light
them on fire and use them to burn the walls of our fort.
We defeated them a second time and killed many of
them including their Seneca chief. A few of our men
decapitated their chief's body and displayed his head
on the top of the palisade.

The Iroquois launched a third attack which we
successfully repulsed. A few Iroquois were sent up the
river by canoe to intercept another war party of five
hundred warriors who were headed to sack Ville-
Marie. They changed their minds and advanced
towards Long Sault arriving on the fifth day of
fighting when our food and ammunition was running
desperately low.

The Huron slaves of the Iroquois shouted to the
Huron loyal to the French inside the fort and
persuaded them to abandon the French. All of the
Huron left us except their chief and a few others. All
but five of them ended up losing their lives in the
battle.

The five hundred Iroquois warriors who had
been previously heading for Ville-Marie arrived and
began to construct mantelets (shields) by lashing three

logs together to protect themselves from our musket fire.

They launched a fourth attack well protected from our musket balls. Our soldiers were exhausted and our food and water were depleted while the Iroquois began hacking through the walls and eventually they began to pour in and climb the walls to attack us from above.

Our commander Dollard ignited a keg of gunpowder which he intended to throw over the stockade onto the Iroquois but it fell against the top of the walls of the fort and bounced back towards him and his men and exploded inside the fort inflicting great casualties. Dollard and the remaining men were quickly overpowered and killed with the exception of the five Huron who somehow survived to tell us what happened.

In any case the Iroquois abandoned their plans to go east and attack our colony in masse. Perhaps they decided if so few of us could withstand such an onslaught for so long so fiercely, it wasn't worth the risk. Or maybe they were disheartened by the decapitation of their chief. Their ways are not our ways and very difficult to decipher. I opine that it was a miracle performed by Our Blessed Mother who protected our little town that is named for her and remains very close to her heart.

Renée insists that we should take advantage of the beautiful early fall afternoon weather and go take a walk together. I don't put up a protest since I'm anxious to switch the conversation and coax him into revealing his feelings. We head for the river's edge where the sun is dancing on the calm crystal blue water.

I make the first move by slipping my hand in his and looking up into those gorgeous blue eyes. He clasps his strong arms around my waist and lifts me off the ground and kisses me as if he hasn't kissed another woman since me four years ago. It's obvious that this dear man has no intention of letting me slip through his grasp again and I'm putty in those hands after that indescribable kiss. He's no longer the shy retiring man I remember as he rapidly relates to me how lost he has been without me and now that I'm no longer married he prays that I would consent to be his wife. Somehow I'm not at all astonished because that kiss laid his heart bare. With all my being shouting yes, yes, yes within me, I agree with a kiss of assent that I know we'll never forget. He needs to be sure if that was a yes, which I realize has yet to leave my mouth. I nod in affirmation and proceed to break into a bout of laughter that was at least a year in arriving! Yes, our lives can be broken to bits, but they can be lifted to new heights of joy as we allow them to mend.

# CHAPTER 21   FULL SPEED AHEAD

We humans were made out of God's love, for love, and we are not truly happy until we find it. Thank you dear Lord for bringing us back together.

Last night Pierre and I agreed there was no point in delaying getting started with our lives together. I admitted there is one thing that has me very concerned. What if I'm permanently sterile? I want you to be able to have a family. He assured me that he was not worried in the slightest that I was rendered permanently infertile because the curse expired with the close of that marriage.

Pierre worries that he could be killed in an ambush and that I would be left alone again. I'm totally willing to assume that risk. I realize that his profession places him in peril, but our whole existence in this besieged colony is fragile with no guarantee of a tomorrow for any of us. All the more reason to grasp happiness while it lies before us. I suggest we give this all over to the Lord, who is the actual architect of our lives. Pierre agrees and then we seal our determination with a kiss.

The next day is September thirteenth, two weeks after the annulment was signed and time to talk with Governor Maisonneuve about arranging to have Pierre Gadois fulfill the terms of our marriage contract signed more than three years ago. The governor agrees that I'm entitled to one hundred livres to be paid on the feast of Sainte-Michel, September twenty-ninth and another three hundred livres on Christmas Day, as an indemnity for the time I lived with him, based on a provision in our contract that would give me a rent of 60 livres, plus an additional three-hundred livres in the event we had no children. He will order him to pay this to me to satisfy our contract stipulations and there is nothing else required on my part.

Our governor is such a kind man and he gingerly ventured to inquire about my future plans. I am thrilled to share the fantastic news that I have consented to marry Pierre Martin dit La Rivière very soon. His face lit up in approbation which has made me even more confident that I've chosen very well indeed, not that I'm harboring a single doubt.

He wishes us the very best as I rise to leave his office and head for the fort with a picnic basket filled with a surprise special dinner for Pierre and me to share. Pierre is so glad to see me he drops everything to hurry us out to the dappled shade of his favorite sugar maple tree where there is a  round table waiting for my tablecloth.

I told him we have the governor's blessing on our impending nuptials and I fill him in on the reason for my visit. Now we need to set a date for our marriage contract signing day. I suggest a day in early October might be best since Renée is about to have her first baby any minute now. At this point I hate to leave her alone for any length of time. I gave her a very large bell to ring to summon the neighbors if I'm not there. I'll be pealing that same bell frantically on delivery day since I have no experience whatsoever in birthing a child.

Pierre agrees that October eighth should be perfect. His sergeant major of the garrison Raphael Lambert Closse and his wife Élizabeth Moyen, our very dear friends, have offered to host our party afterwards. They are the proud parents of their second child Jeanne-Cecile born a few months ago. Tragically their first baby, named Élizabeth for her mom, was born prematurely and died the very next day in October, 1658. It took them a very long time to recover from that shock.

I thank God that Lambert and Élizabeth were not affected by the sterility curse that descended upon us, despite their having pronounced their vows with us on our wedding day. I can't think of any two people who are more deserving of every happiness.

I realize that Renée has been alone long enough and I better head for home. Pierre insists upon shepherding me there and chides me for venturing out alone, even though I'm never without my trusty musket. He knows how useless it would be to me if I was ever faced with the enemy. It is the law that every adult must carry a loaded firearm and I'm a law abiding citizen. I'm not about to argue when any stolen moments with him are so precious. How wondrous that he feels exactly the same. My invitation to return for supper is accepted with an ear to ear smile that reveals those beguiling dimples. He follows that up with an ardent kiss that will have to hold me for a few hours.

Renée is resting as I tiptoe in, relieved that she hasn't required any help in my absence. I get right to picking, peeling and chopping fresh vegetables from the garden for stew so it will be done in time. Ascertaining his favorite meal is impossible since he loves absolutely everything. A sweet pie, everyone's favorite, has been cooling since early this morning and is ready and waiting for dessert. Sometimes I wish we could eat that yummy treat first.

Two days later Renée is sure today is the day, so I spend the time scurrying around like a chipmunk not knowing exactly what I should be doing. I decide to run to the neighbors, who Renée feels are most competent, to warn them that we'll be in need of their help very soon.

This town is in dire need of a mid-wife. We ladies could keep her busier than anyone wishes to be. This is probably why there haven't been any volunteers surfacing. We are also still under a curfew instituted by the governor that no one can be out of our homes past nightfall for our own safety from the Iroquois.

The expectant father Jean returns from work nervous as a cat and ravenous. He gobbles down his meal and I bet if I asked him what he just ate he wouldn't remember! I know how he feels right now, in suspense and not being able to help at all. Renée will have to do all the hard work by herself. Like clockwork her labor begins shortly before dark and stretches into the wee hours of the morning. Jean and I run into each other pacing and praying. It's such a helpless feeling overlaid with the most wonderful anticipation. I just have to go into their bedroom and hold her hand at least, while trying to stay out of the way. Poor Renée's pain is so intense and constant it can't be long now, and I'm right.

I have the happy task of telling Jean he is the father of a beautiful baby boy. He names him Mathurin, after his cousin, and begins to dance around the room in delight that his first child is a boy, as any man would! Renée is exhausted but very relieved it is all over, as she holds and kisses her precious gift from our loving God. It is September sixteenth, 1660 and little Mathurin Valiquet will be baptized later today at Notre Dame Church.

I'm staying home to help Renée recover her strength, happy to be of some use now. Pierre pops his head in to have a look at the little one to make sure he is alright. Surgeons take care of us from birth until we head to the Hotel-Dieu which is basically only for the dying among us. He pronounces him absolutely perfect which is a mighty relief to all. I cannot wait to play the role of mother to our own little one, our very own little miracle.

# CHAPTER 22   ONE CRUCIAL STEP CLOSER

Caring for mother and baby, who are doing very well, has fully occupied the last three weeks with all our friends and neighbors making visits bearing gifts of food and lovely handmade presents.

Pierre has been our most frequent visitor which has pleased and delighted me. Funny how he always coincides his "just dropping by to check on the baby" with the supper hour.

I haven't had the time to give much thought to our engagement party/marriage contract signing day. Thank goodness Élizabeth and Lambert are handling it at their place. I'll wear Pierre's favorite bright red dress, which he says is my best color and his favorite color for this most joyful occasion.

This is an essential step to take before saying our vows. Another is Father Gabriel Souart will announce the banns of marriage over the next three Sundays at Mass. The banns of marriage in church canon law reads: "If any of you know cause or just impediment why these two persons should not be joined together in Holy Matrimony you are to declare it."

If there is anyone left in town that hasn't heard our plans to marry they'll finally get the word. I know there has been plenty of gossip about the two of us, especially me. "How could I be so daring as to marry so soon, and just who do I think I am!" No one will actually say anything directly to me because they know how I'd react. Those people have proven they aren't my true friends, so I really don't care what they say.

I know I need to get on with my life because I'll be turning eighteen in a few months and not getting any younger. These are prime baby making years that are going to waste. It's quite obvious that Pierre agrees with me. He is so anxious to fill his home with my contented singing as I go about my work and the laughter of our children echoing from the rafters. His dreams for the future coincide with mine perfectly.

It's the morning of October eighth, another golden autumn day as Pierre arrives at the home to accompany me and Jean to Notary Basset's office to sign our marriage contract. We are greeted by an amazing raucous contingent of our friends at his office door before we enter for the solemn business of marriage contract signing.

Notary Basset reads to us the following:
**Marriage Contract: Marie Pontonnier & Pierre Martin dit La Rivière**

Before etc., appeared in their persons Pierre Martin dit La Riviere, son of the late Jacques Martin and Simone Clousteau, his father and mother, from the parish of Sainte Colombe in the land of Anjou on one side and Marie Pontonnier, daughter of the late Urbain Pontonnier and Felicité Jamin, her father and mother, from the town of Le Lude in the land of Anjou on the other side. In the presence of and with the consent of their relatives and friends assembled for this on either side, that is: on the part of the said Pierre Martin: Master Jean Gervaise, Nicholas Millet, Urbain Brossard, Pierre Desaulets, Jean Beaudoin, Laurent Archambault and Pierre Barreau. And on the part of the said Marie Pontonnier: Jean Valliquet, dit La Verdure, her paternal cousin; Mathurin Langevin, Sieur de La Croix; Raphael Lambert Closse, squire, sergeant major of the garrison of the said place; Master Charles Lemoyne, merchant and Jacques LeBer, also a merchant in the said place all regular friends of the said parties. [Which parties] acknowledge and admit having made the treaties and promises of marriage that follows: Be it known that the said Martin has promised to take the said Marie Pontonnier as his wife and legitimate spouse, as also the said Marie Pontonnier has promised to take the said Pierre Martin as her husband and legitimate spouse, the marriage to be celebrated and  solemnized in the Holy Roman Catholic Apostolic Church as soon as is able and that it shall be decided and discussed between them and their said relatives and friends if God and our Holy Mother Church give their consent and accord, to be one and united in all goods acquired before and during their marriage, according to the custom of the Prévoté and viscounty of Paris followed and maintained in this country. The said future groom shall take the said future bride with her rights, names, reasons and actions in whatever places that they may be situated, located and found. The said future bride shall be given the customary dower according to the said custom. The said future spouses are in accord with their said relatives and friends that the said future bride shall preferentially take before the division of the estate after the death of the said future groom out of the goods of the said community the sum of three hundred livres which she has promised and obligated to bring to the said [community] which sum shall remain the property of her and hers. The future spouses have reserved the faculty of making each other a mutual donation in case there be no children born of their said future marriage and have promised to be agreeable to the present contract and not to contravene it. Such has been agreed between their relatives and friends, made and passed in the said Ville-Marie in the study of the notary in the year one thousand six hundred sixty, the eighth day of October before noon in the presence of Sieurs Jacques Lemoyne, Nicholas millet, Jean Boudoin, Jehan Gervaise, U. Broussard, Desaulets (with flourish), Basset, notary

Notary Basset congratulates us, commenting that he thinks we have the largest group of witnesses he's ever had in his office and that this bodes well for a long and happy marriage ahead. A cheer goes up from our friends in approval. We thank him and file out with Sergeant major Lambert Closse leading the way to the party he and Élizabeth have prepared in our honor. Some of the men depart to fetch their wives so they may attend the festivities also.

I wish Renée could join us but she decided it was best to stay home with the baby. Mothers of newborns are understandably hesitant to bring their young ones into large gatherings for fear of contracting a disease. Also nursing mothers have problems finding a quiet place to feed their babies.

Élizabeth and Lambert have laid out enough scrumptious looking food to feed a battalion of hungry soldiers. It tastes every bit as good as it looks. How much I appreciate not having to lift a finger to prepare any of it.

After we have all eaten much more than our fill, we split up and the men head outside to smoke their pipes and talk about whatever men like to talk about. While inside the ladies rest for a time and talk about our impending wedding which is set for November third. The weather is the biggest problem since it probably will be very cold by then so a church yard reception is out.

Élizabeth insists that we should have the reception in their spacious barn. It can accommodate everyone and still have room for dancing which is a must have for every French wedding. I am beyond grateful for this wonderful offer. We had been trying to whittle down our guest list to a handful of friends so they could fit in Pierre's little house. We were bound to offend three quarters of our friends in the process. Pierre has befriended so many residents of our little town in his work.

A barn dance is the perfect solution to our dilemma and since we want to have a more casual wedding anyway, it's perfect. I decide to run outside to tell Pierre since I know it's been on his mind. He thanks Lambert profusely for his kind offer especially since we have just been feted by him and Élizabeth in such an extraordinary fashion. He says it has been his pleasure and we should all get together like this more often. I secretly say a fervent prayer that this is my second and last marriage contract signing party.

# CHAPTER 23   TO LOVE AND TO CHERISH

As I dress this wedding day morning of November third I should not be comparing how I feel today to my previous experience but it is difficult to refrain from doing just that. My heart is bursting with joy as I contemplate a fresh start with the most sweet and humble man. For we have grown more in love, with every day we've spent together.

That is how it should be, two people coming together like two vines in the forest intertwining to form the strongest rope, impossible to separate yet respectful of the others need to grow and thrive.

I think I've matured quite a bit since I first landed on the shores of this untamed land four and a half years ago. My girlish streak of self-centeredness has hopefully been erased never to return. I know Pierre's profession will force me to share him with all the citizens of this town so there is simply no room for any selfish tendencies.

The beautiful new wedding dress that my dearest friend Élizabeth lovingly made me is the most beautiful shade of periwinkle blue abundantly festooned with pure white Chantilly lace. It is such a shame that I must cover it with my navy blue heavy wool cape with hood for the walk to the church.

At the front door Pierre makes the most charming picture of the proud groom, his countenance beaming. The snow that began falling at dawn dusting his vibrant red coat and hat topped off with a jaunty pheasant feather. He is accompanied by most of his friends who are similarly attired. Jean, Renée and tiny Mathurin who is wrapped up so as to totally shield him from any snowflakes are coming along also. So off we head to church gleefully singing a sprightly marching tune accompanied by a fiddle and drum.

Father Gabriel Souart greets us at the open church door, while inside await the rest of our friends who had wisely decided to take refuge inside. Our musical procession headed by Pierre march down the aisle and I pull up the rear alone a few paces behind. I carry my well-worn prayer book trimmed with white ribbons and lace in lieu of the flowers that were cut down by the recent hard frost.

Pierre waits with Father before the altar where vases filled with pine boughs and other greenery tied with blue and white satin bows flank the tabernacle on the back wall. We take our places before the prié dieus facing the altar and the Holy Sacrifice of the Mass begins. After the Gloria there are readings from the Old and New Testaments. Then Father delivers a lovely sermon about how the love of the bride and groom is a reflection of God's love for and union with all of us, the members of His Body the Church. It's now time to pronounce our vows to "love and to cherish until death do us part." We both declare this in loud and clear voices so even our friends in the back pew can hear us.

Father proceeds with the rest of the Mass beginning with the Nicene Creed and enters into the solemn consecration of the bread and wine into the Body and Blood of our Savior, Jesus Christ. Everyone receives the Holy Eucharist and then pray quietly in thanksgiving for His unfathomable gift of Himself to us, His unworthy children. Father pronounces a special Nuptial Blessing over us and then blesses the entire congregation and our wedding ceremony is concluded.

We thank Father and invite him to our dinner reception in the Closses' barn which he enthusiastically accepts. As we turn to face all of our smiling family and friends I feel an overwhelming sense of gratitude and relief that now our lives and love are united. We lead the way back down the aisle, through the doors and as we cross the threshold we pause to kiss and hug each other for the first time as husband and wife.

Then off we march again through the lightly falling snow accompanied by the stalwart musicians to the big red barn in the distance. I'm glad there are so many of us to warm up the barn with our body heat. However I know that once we get to dancing all thought of the cold will melt away. Pierre and I make the rounds of the tables meeting and greeting as everyone is eating their dinner and then we partake and drink from our special two-handled cup. After a few sincere toasts to us over our dessert of sweet pies the musicians strike up the music. Pierre and I set the vibrant spectrum of colors to swirling as we dance above the sweet fresh hay spread on the dirt floor of the barn. The children join in the fun with their typical abandon.

I get to dance with every one of the gentlemen in attendance at least once. Some are better dancers than the others but what they lack in skill, they more than make up for in enthusiasm. I discover there are no shy men in our village if this group is any indication. The time goes so quickly when you are so enjoyably occupied with folks who wish you the best.

I corral Pierre who has just noticed it is time to depart as dusk has arrived and everyone needs to get safely home very soon. He disappears for a few moments as I say good bye to as many friends as I can. To my surprise Pierre has lead his very large dappled gray horse from behind the barn and opened the large doors. He then carefully boosts me up on to Brutus and then swings himself up behind me to the cheers of all and off we gallop into the sunset like characters in a storybook.

# CHAPTER 24   LOVE NESTING

Who would have ever imagined on last New Year's day, when I was immersed in the misery of a dissolving marriage with no way out of the morass, that I would be preparing for a joyous holiday season with my precious husband at the close of that same year. I want to make our first holidays together as memorable as my imagination can create for my wonderful man. We are still honeymooning which I realize is more than enough for him. I'm enjoying making hearty and delicious foods for him and transforming this long time bachelor abode into a cozy home.

We don't have a large piece of land or farm to tend because he simply didn't have the time to devote to it, but there is room for an adequate vegetable garden that I can't wait to plant in the spring. In the meantime during this winter maybe I'll grow in proficiency with a needle and thread so I can make clothes for the babies that we're planning and praying for.

I'm doing my level best not to fret about it and just relax. We French women have the reputation for great fertility. The men who originally came to build this colony thought the Indian women would make good mates and could match our pregnancy rate but soon found out that for the village to grow rapidly they better import women from back in France. I've noticed that the Indian women nurse their babies for a very long time, and this may be the reason for their smaller families.

Renée and Jean want to host the Reveillon Feast after Christmas Midnight Mass this year, so I will be working with her side by side to prepare it. She is still nursing three month old Mathurin and is very concerned about bringing him out into the frigid air for Mass so that's improbable. She can stay home with him and make sure our Yule Log keeps burning strong and the dinner hot.

They have invited several bachelor friends who I understand have been talking about the feast like little boys since the day they were first invited so it just better be outstanding. Hopefully we can satisfy their vaulted expectations. I welcome this opportunity to treat Élizabeth and Lambert and their little Jeanne-Cecile for a change. As our best friends they will always be considered part of our family.

Jean's cousin Mathurin Langevin dit La Croix and his wife Marie Renaud will also be in attendance. Renée's cousin Pierre Raguideau dit Sainte-Germain and his wife Marguerite Rebours and their precious little one Marie-Angelique who was baptized while the bishop was in town on August twenty-second will join us also. I realize there is no way that all of these folks would ever fit in our home. Our family will definitely need to relocate in the near future so there will be room for our children.

Planning and carrying out this yearly extravaganza is not for the faint of heart, but is always worth the total exhaustion that inevitably follows. I just pray I don't nod off to sleep in church as so many women have been known to do. I don't want to miss even one second of this magnificent Christmas Midnight Mass or I risk being counted among Jesus' apostles who couldn't remain awake in prayer for even one hour during His agony in the Garden of Gethsemane. If I can't be counted on to share in the overwhelming joy of the celebration of His Coming into this unworthy world, how will I ever withstand the grief we all must endure in this life. What we are asked to bear is but a pale reflection of His excruciating journey. We should take heart in our Lord's words to his disciples when He found them sleeping. "The spirit is willing, but the flesh is weak." Our lives are a testing ground we must traverse if we are to enter into His Glory in the next world. For each one of us is called to be a saint in our Father's eyes, whose opinion is the only one that counts. Jesus has commanded "Be you therefore perfect as your heavenly Father is perfect."

In compiling their guest list I can't help but notice the absence of single women for the ever hopeful bachelors. This year only three filles à marier arrived in the whole colony of Québec. We were lucky to receive one girl, but our need remains great if we are to grow. Last year was a banner year in comparison, with eighteen young women coming to Ville-Marie, fourteen to Québec City and two to Trois-Rivières. I've heard there is an extraordinarily unfortunate misapprehension in France that the females that are coming here are prostitutes! I can attest that this is a reprehensible rumor that has taken hold, because we women are the antithesis of that. We are highly devout God-fearing Catholic women raising fine families of excellent repute. I understand that the Governor will be sending an emissary to our King, who is expressing more interest in our colony's development, to counter these charges sometime this coming year. That move should improve our image and increase our immigration substantially. Malicious gossip and innuendo can damage the reputations of innocent persons. Now an entire population of good women has been maligned.

As the big day approaches, I put the last touches on my present for Pierre, a bright blue knitted sweater, hat, scarf and mittens since I think that color brings out those big blue eyes. I inserted a stripe of his favorite red to please him. Today, I've been singing Christmas carols while decking our love nest with fresh pine and spruce boughs, pine cones, red ribbons and candles. I've found there are too many spruce boughs so I decide to fashion them into a large wreath tied together with wire and for the finishing touch a large red bow at the top and lean this circle against the stone wall in the middle upon the boughs spread on the mantelpiece. Their refreshing scent fills the air with that evocative fragrance that only the twelve days of Christmas possess.

The wonderful smell immediately harkens me back to my childhood and reminds me to unpack the most important component, the crèche and nestle it prominently on the mantelpiece among the greens. I hope that soon it will be placed in a more easily accessible spot on the table where our first child can place a piece of straw in the manger for each good deed he or she has done every day of the Advent season.

I light the candles for Pierre to see through the window as he comes home from a long day of rounds around the village. His work regrettably increases as the winter temperatures deepen and the population contracts various illnesses from the common cold to consumption. Please dear Lord, preserve his health. He arrives and leads trusty Brutus into the small paddock in the back, waters and feeds him there, where he will get some much deserved rest for the night.

Pierre enters by the back door and is greeted by the competing smells of hot soup, fresh baked bread, Christmas greens and candles. He is one happy man, eager to show me just how much by kissing me passionately while he lifts me off the floor and spins me round and round like a rag doll. He puts me down and declares that the long ride home breathing all that fresh cold air have left him famished and the smells wafting from our fireplace are just too tempting to resist. I would add "frisky" to his description of himself but first we must say grace to God for His many blessings and partake of the hot soup that's been simmering for hours above the fire.

# CHAPTER 25 CAN IT BE?

The flint-tipped arrow glistens as it slices between the white birch trees like a razor, piercing the crimson wool of the rider, who slumps forward over his silent musket. Oh my dear God, it is Pierre on Brutus! I must reach him.

I awake gasping for air and roll from our bed. Shivering in the late February darkness, drenched in a cold sweat, I grab my robe at the foot of the bed and search in the blackness for my slippers. I must exit without disturbing him because he can't find out what I just witnessed. I'll go light the fire and warm my bones. Please Lord may he sleep in a bit this morning until I regain my composure. I must have time to think.

Is this a precognitive dream, or a nightmare conjured up by my subconscious which knows that we face this menace, this possible cruel end every single day? I must go see Élizabeth today. No, on second thought maybe she is still raw from her parents' massacre and she also faces the same worry about her warrior husband. No, I'll unload this on Renée and pray she can keep this secret. She gave birth to her first child Mathurin in September. I'd love to have him as a diversion today.

I'm so very afraid this is a warning from above, a way to prepare me for the imminent eventuality of his death. This dream was so clear, so vivid, completely silent except for the twang of the bowstring as it launched the arrow on its deadly mission. How many times will I relive this vision before we part?

I need to pray to Jesus that He will erase this for I'm not ready to lose him. That would be beyond my capacity to endure. No it just cannot happen. I will storm the heavens for the help of my Mother Mary. Please preserve him for I love him so! Mama, Papa, my Guardian Angel surround him with an impenetrable shield. I will send out my angel every day to help guard him as he makes his rounds. Lord have mercy on us, Christ have mercy on us, Lord have mercy on us!

Pierre had feared this, which made him hesitant to propose marriage to me. He had a feeling that he might die in an ambush and leave me alone once again and it would be more than I could bear. My fervent love outweighed my fear, at that time, so few short months ago.

Well I hear Pierre stirring so I better get breakfast. I send him off with trepidation hidden by a big smile and set off to Renée's in the opposite direction. She welcomes my early visit and we manage to spend a lovely morning together despite my revelation. There is something about babies that can brighten anybody's mood. She reminded me that there is nothing we can do but wake up every morning with joy in our hearts for the gift of another day, for if we allow ourselves to slip into maudlin thoughts we will miss the happiness the present moment holds.

I return to our little house with a bounce in my step, which isn't easy in snowshoes on deeply drifting snow. Next on the agenda is preparing supper for my hungry man. I'm suddenly very tired so I might lie down while the pot simmers and have a nap. It's been a draining day with a very early start and Pierre won't be home for awhile.

I'm awakened with a kiss, a big smile from my love and the most startling pronouncement. "I think you might be pregnant, darling!" That makes me sit bolt upright. "Do you think it is possible Pierre?! I have been feeling more easily tired lately." "Well it's early yet, but that is a definite sign. I hate to jump to conclusions and end up being wrong, but I just feel that you are." "Well, let's have dinner right now because I think I'm as hungry as you are!"

# CHAPTER 26   LET IT SNOW, LET IT SNOW, LET IT SNOW

The first three weeks of March, we were blessed with what seemed like everlasting blizzards! I was content to be snowed in with Pierre as we made plans for our new arrival. My nightmare faded into the distance as I wove cloth and knitted a layette. We don't care a bit whether the baby I am carrying is a girl or a boy, just healthy and strong, please God. The arrival date will be sometime in November so plenty of warm clothes will be needed.

All of my friends were informed right away since I just couldn't keep this a secret. Every last one of them read my face and knew at first sight I was a woman transformed, just glowing with the aura of impending motherhood. This will be the longest wait, but we can use these months to prepare and pray for a perfect miracle.

Pierre decided he needed a new pastime and he would try his hand at cooking. Like every expectant father with his first child on the way he was treating me like a fragile princess. His first efforts were comical to say the least but turned out edible nonetheless. Cooking and baking is all trial and error, and one will never learn if not left alone to make these mistakes. This was probably not the best time to begin since we were socked in with snow and supplies were running a little low. Nothing would deter him from his new assignment, for Frenchmen are the most stubborn of their species. He was determined to learn this or die trying!

On March twenty-fourth we could finally open the back door so Pierre could squeeze out. Both Brutus and Pierre were raring to go and in dire need of a workout. The five foot icicles hanging from the roof all around were crashing to the snow beneath, shattering into enormous glass like chunks. It was an annual ritual, yet ever new, since the thaw varies considerably from year to year. Pierre was torn about leaving me alone, but I insisted that he get out and make his long neglected rounds, starting with the fort.

Meanwhile I need to catch up with some work around the house that has accumulated during our long but lovely confinement. I've promised to take a nice long nap this afternoon. I'm taking back the reins in the cooking and baking department which I've missed so much, however if he wants to do the dishes after supper I won't complain.

Today I plan to make him a nice big flaky meat pie which just happens to be his favorite dish. I'll bake it this morning so it won't have a chance to burn while I take my nap. This pie must be as perfect as I can make it and I should bake a few loaves of bread and a delectable maple sugar pie for dessert at the same time.

How blissfully happy I am at this moment in time! What more could I desire than the man of my dreams by my side and his baby on the way. I raise the roof with my singing as I knead the dough for the bread and pie crusts. What wonderful smells fill the house and waft up the chimney as I retrieve the bubbling pies. It will take all of my willpower to refrain from sampling them before dinner.

Oh, my goodness I've slept a long time! It is very dark and the coals in the fireplace have died way down. Maybe Pierre is rubbing down Brutus in the shed. By the dim light of my lantern I find Brutus in the back waiting patiently in the cold, but where, oh where is Pierre? I examine our dear steed carefully and ask him where he could be. On closer inspection I find blood on his saddle and blanket. Maybe I'm in a horrific nightmare and any minute I'll wake up in our bed next to my love. Oh, my dear sweet Jesus wake me up soon because this just can't be true, my nightmare of a month ago can't have come to pass.

# CHAPTER 27  PRAY AND SEARCH

After an interminable night of waiting, crying, and praying in the dark in the corner rocker all alone, I decided to depart for the fort on foot at first light. I couldn't bring myself to even touch Brutus' bloody saddle and blanket for now. I contemplated whether I should walk beside Brutus in case anything on him would be of the slightest assistance to them but decided that was foolish. He would be waiting in his paddock if anyone would like to use him in the search. Brutus knew well where his home and food were located, but I seriously doubt whether he could retrace his steps to his master.

I couldn't eat breakfast or for that matter supper the night before. Had a quick cup of tea and set off in haste shod in my snowshoes and heavy cape. Our dearest friend Major Lambert Closse heard my cries on my approach and ran out to meet me. His stricken face set off another torrent from me as I choked out my dire news. His dearest friend and the town's only surgeon is missing and may have succumbed to an Iroquois ambush.

He organized a posse in a flash and accompanied me to his home on his trusty steed so that Élizabeth could care for me. I think I was still in shock as he helped me off his horse into her arms and the warmth of their home. As she resumed feeding little Jeanne-Cecile I told her what happened last night and the nightmare I'd had a month ago, which despite my most fervent pleas to our Lord has probably been fulfilled.

We share a pot of tea prepared on the marvelous new invention of a cast iron woodstove. Pierre and I have one on order that we plan to install in our new home this spring. I pick at the lovely breakfast she insists I try to consume. She chides me for concealing my nightmare from her but understands how thoughtful I was to consider her experience of the loss of both her parents and their home to an Iroquois massacre. She still has recurrent nightmares of that horrific day when her husband saved both her and her younger sister from slaughter.

Thank goodness she survived to marry and give birth to this precious little one who so resembles her lovely mother. Lambert and she still mourn the loss of their first baby.

We both relate our experiences during the last three weeks of unprecedented white-out blizzards which almost totally covered all the tiny windows of the second floor of the homes in the village and served to protect us from Iroquois incursions. Élizabeth told me the most amazing story of our new heroine Barbe Poisson who last month during a February surprise attack of one hundred-fifty Iroquois fearlessly took an armful of muskets to our French settlers as a band of Iroquois were invading from every direction as far as her home. She was able to reach them just as they were being pursued and handed off the weapons to Monsieur Le Moyne just in the nick of time. The weapons were crucial to the settlers' ability to hold the enemy at bay.

I so wish I'd known about this event because those irate Iroquois must be lying in wait on the outskirts of Montréal. One of them may have picked off my dearest Pierre as he went to visit those same settlers. Oh, dear God may our search party find him alive or perhaps the Iroquois seized him to hold him as a hostage. Last year in Trois-Rivières a nine year old girl named Anne Baillargeon was kidnapped. Her parents still hold out hope that she will return to them.

Despite all the tea I'm quite exhausted and succumb to Élizabeth's suggestion that I lie down for a nap. I'm almost afraid to close my eyes for fear of what I might see in my dreams. Why, oh why did I send him out, perhaps to his death? I'll never forgive myself if the worst is true and our dear sweet baby has to grow up without a father. I dissolve in tears once more and cry myself to sleep like a little child.

What a blessing, when I awake I can't remember any dreams good or otherwise and it appears dusk is upon us. I want to help Élizabeth prepare supper and pick up some tips on the intricacies of cooking and baking with a woodstove. It will be a good diversion, anything to distract myself from reality. Jeanne-Cecile is babbling away to her mama and has learned to stay away from the hot surfaces of the stove all around. What a darling she is, so sweet and quiet. She has persuaded me that maybe I'd like to have a girl for my first. Think what a marvelous help she will be to her mom with the younger babies that will be coming along. That is the advantage of having such large loving families, the older ones are such a great help with the household and farm chores and each child helps to keep watch over the next born right on down the line to the youngest.

There is still no news, but Lambert promised to return for supper and night curfew so he should arrive soon since dinner is almost ready and it's quite dark.

He arrived with his head hanging low and his solemn expression unchanged. He gave me a reassuring hug as he slumped down into his seat at the head of the table. We joined hands and said grace "In the name of the Father and the Son and the Holy Ghost. Bless us, oh Lord and these Thy gifts which we are about to receive from Thy bounty through Christ our Lord. Amen."

They searched beginning at our home where they fetched Brutus for our excellent Onodaga tracker to ride. They retraced his steps stopping along the way to speak to each family on Pierre's route to tell them and ascertain where he was headed to next, and repeated this all the way along. I remembered that I neglected to tell him about my dream of the arrow flying through a grove of white birch trees to pierce Pierre in the back. We have a plethora of beautiful white birch trees dotting our town so that is not much help.

Tonight's falling snow is obliterating any clues that remain for tomorrow's search, and the thought of him out there somewhere slowly being covered with snow in the frigid night air is more than I can bear. I excuse myself and retreat to the guest room to cry alone. "Why dear Lord have you sent me this cross to bear alone, so soon after we found such happiness? I know I'm not alone, there is his child growing within me and the best friends any one could possibly have. How is it that I feel You have abandoned me?"

# CHAPTER 28  LIMBO

The next morning, after a tormented nightmarish night, little Jeanne-Cecile peeks at me over the mattress' edge and offers me her favorite rag doll which I take and hold to my chest. She lights up with delight at my reception of her gift and babbles a sweet greeting. Visualizing my own dear baby doing the same next year melts my broken heart. I scoop her up to join me and cuddle her close. This early morning reverie serves as a tonic to face another day of waiting, wondering and watching the horizon.

She decides it is time to rise and I return her dolly as we bounce off the featherbed. She wants to rejoin her mom immediately so I can only grab my robe and slippers. I am so surprised to find near the hearth around the table all my dearest friends including Renée who kisses and hugs me tight and begins to cry which sets us all off for a time. Élizabeth quickly brings a couple of pots of tea and hot biscuits to spread with berry preserves.

With a look of bewilderment on the baby's tiny sweet face in response to our torrent of tears, Jeanne-Cecile climbs into my lap and proffers her doll once more to comfort me. How does she know that I'm the nexus of all this fuss? How very perceptive she is for one so tiny. What a blessing little ones are to us grownups who need to be reminded just how fragile life is and how our very existence in this place and time is a miracle for which we owe Him our gratitude, no matter the circumstances, in joy and sorrow. I know I must bear this weighty cross for this period of time and must ask Him for His help in carrying it for He will never forsake me. His love never fails us for even a second, for if it did, we would cease to exist.

After just a short visit, at times a bit strained, for which I express my sincere appreciation there are kisses and hugs all around. They bundle up, put on their snowshoes and gather up their muskets to head for hearth and home under a threatening sky. I'm afraid regrettably they all have a renewed sense of awareness and dread now that they've learned from Élizabeth the harrowing story of Barbe Poisson and her unbelievably heroic action in Trois-Rivière a few weeks ago which saved many souls from certain death, along with my sad vigil for Pierre. I am so thankful for their summoning up the courage to leave their nests now that it is painfully obvious that the Iroquois have stepped up their war upon us.

I so wish the fashion in our homeland for beaver pelt hats would wane soon and that possibly would relieve the carnage in our colony. How very ironic and tragic that the sin of greed so propels both sides. They are not interested in the tiny spot of land we occupy. They covet those pelts and must eliminate their competition at all cost. How ludicrous that my Pierre probably has perished so that some wealthy person in France can sport a fine beaver pelt hat!

Our afternoon was spent in quiet contemplation, both of us lost in our thoughts and prayers as we rhythmically plied the thread of the spinning wheel and pumped the treadle of the loom. Jeanne-Cecile played silently with her dolls until naptime came for both of us. I find that I'm more tired than usual from accumulated stress and the foreboding skies that herald more snow before nightfall.

Élizabeth insists that she has dinner under control and I should succumb to nature's call to sleep. I'm unable to hold open my eyelids any longer and while rocking Jeanne-Cecile on my lap we both drift off. Surprisingly she awakens first and gently arouses me with a kiss and tug on my hand. This little one has totally won my heart and unknowingly managed to distract me from my unrelenting grief, like an angel sent down from heaven. What would I do without those big brown eyes looking up at me under that halo of golden curls, tugging my hand, tugging my heart. She will surely become my child's best friend in this life, just as her mom is mine.

She spies her father in the distance as he approaches through the falling snow. She cries out with glee and runs to her mom to announce him with a delighted exclamation of "Papa, papa!"

He joins us with an obviously heavy heart, worn down with grief, heightened by his necessary repetition of his sad story to all of his good friends throughout the territory. He apologized to me with tears flooding his eyes that he had reached the last family who saw Pierre a couple of hours ago.

## CHAPTER 29  HELP IN HEALING

"Where to go from here?" is the question I must grapple with now that Lambert has had to call off the search after five more unproductive days. I know in my heart he is not coming home to me, and he awaits me in heaven with Mama and Papa. They were there to welcome him and give him a tour of his new abiding place. For as Saint Paul says "Eye hath not seen, nor ear heard, neither hath it entered into the heart of man, what things God hath prepared for those who love Him". 1 Corinthians 2:9. My Pierre loved Him ardently and showed Him every day in his tireless work for others who needed him and miss him now. Maybe our Father was in need of another caring soul up there.

I wish I'd had more time to learn skills from him because I think the best use of my time now while I wait for the return of his remains and the birth of our child is to go back to where I began this adventure. I will rejoin Jeanne Mance and the dear sisters at the hospital and help them in any way I can. She has invited me to live there where it is safer for a pregnant woman living alone and hopefully I will feel useful. Maybe they need another pair of hands in the kitchen.

The marriageable girls that arrived in 1659 were eighteen strong, but in the spring of 1660 only one intrepid soul chose Montréal.  So regrettably I probably will not be needed to mentor any new arrivals. I'm sure the number this coming spring will be zero once news of the increased Iroquois incursions reaches France. Few will be foolish enough to embark on what could prove to be a suicide mission.

This is a very sad time for me and our entire colony of Québec. We desperately need help from the King if we are to survive. It is our prayer he soon shows some interest in helping us here in the New World or we will be snuffed out and it will not be for want of excellent stalwart men and women of the bravest caliber. It will be neglect and indifference on the part of the King and his advisors that will be responsible for our grave losses and the missed opportunity to thrive here. Now that's quite enough about my frustrations with politics.

My cousin Jean and his wife Renée want me to come for a visit now and help her with their first child Mathurin who was baptized September 16, 1660 and is now six months old. Another welcome invitation and diversion from my troubles is most appreciated. I have an excellent rapport with Renée who I mentored as soon as I knew she intended to marry Jean. We remain quite close, like sisters, but ones who don't squabble. Their Mathurin is a delightful little one and we will all have a good time as we impatiently wait for spring to arrive. April and all of springtime is usually very unpredictable weather wise.

I know it must sound as if I'm in denial and reluctant to embrace the reality of Pierre's passing and that I should let myself go and sink in the mire, but my situation of pregnancy after so long a wait is taking the edge off the blade. My firm foundation in my faith in the Lord's plan for us, my child and me, and the fact that I must think of the good of the baby places my health in a place of top priority right now for that was always Pierre's wish.

Maybe the fact that they still have not found his body has left a glimmer of the tiniest hope shining a minute light for me. The reality that we haven't placed my dearest in the ground adds to this false hope. Even if they were to find him, the earth is still too frozen solid to dig a hole for his grave. This is another strange aspect of living at such a far north locale. Bodies are always stored until the month of May for burial, placing an odd interlude between stages of grief. Perhaps this serves to usher us along gently in the grieving process or does this serve to reopen the wound just as it has begun to heal? In my case this remains to be seen so taking just one day at a time is the way for me to proceed just as I did when I lost Papa. It seems to be a repeating refrain of my life that I'm knocked to the ground and must pick myself up, brush myself off, and start all over again.

# CHAPTER 30   RETURN TO THE HOTEL-DIEU

My return to my starting place was all that I hoped and so much more. Jeanne Mance welcomed the "grown up" me with as much love as the first day I set eyes on her by the dock that bright summer day five years ago. The three sisters of Saint Joseph, Sisters Bresolle, Mace and Maillet, were delighted to have me join them in their wonderful work. They were so very sorry that I'm left wondering if Pierre survived the attack and assured me that they have been besieging the Lord to give us an answer soon so my mind can rest knowing what has happened to him. They were all surprised and thrilled at my happy news that I'm pregnant! I'm sure that if the Queen Mother of France were to appear at their door she would not have been treated any more royally than I.

The scrumptious dinner they prepared in my honor was fit for a king. I exclaimed that I was eating for two now not a battalion of soldiers. They were hearing none of it and insisted I eat another slice of pie. It was good to be back but I was determined that they should go to no additional trouble for me, for I am just another member of their family for the foreseeable future and a very grateful one at that. I hope to be able to earn my keep because so far my pregnancy has been smooth and I'm feeling very well. They had better put me to work so this time of waiting will fly by. That is exactly what I need right now, their companionship, love and concern along with meaningful work to make me feel needed. Since a woman's work is never done, I don't think that will be a problem.

The next day began quite early at 5:00 which is fine with me. The breakfast we prepared was as bountiful as the banquet from the night before. I was delighted to help feed the patients who find it difficult to feed themselves. It seems to be God's plan that as we grow old and feeble we become like children once again. Although these dear sweet folks seem a bit more cooperative than the babes are. I notice they listen and respect the nuns and are ever so grateful. As for me they react with delighted surprise at the new lady among them who doesn't wear a habit but has her hair pinned back in a practical bun and a long white apron tied around the waist. I'm feeling needed already and am able to momentarily forget my grief as Sister Maillet explains the daily routine. She insists that I take my afternoon nap as usual because the patients certainly always nod off after dinner which is served at noon. I don't argue with her because I'm sure I will be ready for rest after we prepare the food, eat and feed the patients once more.

There are only ten patients in residence right now. They come here to stay when they get too old to take care of themselves and most, sadly, do not have families to provide care for them. There are no formal visiting hours so friends and family can come and go when their schedule permits, which is usually in the late afternoon. The evening supper is served at 5:00

and is a bit lighter than the noontime meal. Many of the older folks don't eat all that much but it is strange how they always have room for dessert or even a second helping.

Absolutely essential to the well-being of both patients and staff are the frequent visits of Father Gabriel Souart. On Sundays he celebrates Mass for the staff and patients right in the dormitory, a very welcome accommodation for all of us. We have a separate tiny chapel in a small room where we can pray before the Blessed Sacrament anytime during the day or night if we like. I love to calm myself with Jesus and pour out my anxieties and fears. He is the best listener but I must work on being quiet so I can hear his replies.

Father Souart is very concerned about me and my unique situation and takes me aside almost daily to listen intently to ascertain how I am actually doing. We have known each other for so long that we have become great friends and I can tell him anything and fool him in nothing. He knows that behind my brave face lies a quivering mass of fear and doubt. The answer to my moving ahead requires a measure of closure which will only come about when Pierre is found. Until then I must be patient and look ahead to the sight of our baby's sweet face. The mere thought of that widens the smile on my countenance once again and fills me with God's peace and contentment. I think I will sleep much better tonight.

# CHAPTER 31   AT LAST

How is it possible, dear Lord, that we are approaching three months since Pierre's disappearance? It is the twenty-second of June, with every trace of snow departed and no one has found him yet! Waiting has become torturous for me no matter how distracted I am with my days full of duties for this dear family of elders I've come to love as my own. Even the sisters are frustrated that the answer remains hanging out there like some "Sword of Damocles" poised to strike.

Help me Lord and forgive my impatience, a virtue which I have learned is almost impossible to achieve. I know it was all in your plan that the delay took me to visit Élizabeth and Renée and their delightful babies that remind me of the joy ahead and the gratitude I have for that incalculable blessing. Then the waiting guided me here with all its attendant blessings I feel every day. If I were to have returned to our home, all alone, who knows how I would have endured? So Your hand holds mine and guides me. Please don't let go Lord, for I fear falling into a well of endless depth. Dear Jesus, thanks for listening and help me fall back to sleep tonight because 5 o'clock will be upon us soon.

One of the sisters must have heard me get up last night and head for the chapel for they all let me sleep in very late this morning. How unusual it feels, almost decadent, but I must have needed a recharge of both body and mind. I think I'm at the half way point in my pregnancy and the baby is beginning to toss around quite a bit, a truly indescribable feeling.

Time to eat and get back to work for I'm sure the sisters and patients have missed me this morning and it's almost time to prepare dinner. They welcome me back to my job as head chef, an honor really not deserved, but when I first arrived Sister Mace decided she would like to retire from that role and placed the hat ceremoniously upon my head. Since then my task has been to live up to their vaulted expectations of me. You'd have to ask the sisters and patients if I have succeeded in transitioning from cooking for two to cooking for fifteen!

After making the rounds greeting and feeding them dinner, there is actually time to catch up on some knitting for the baby instead of taking a nap. The rhythm of the needles is so relaxing and rejuvenating that it has become my very favorite hobby and our little one will be warm and well-dressed if nothing else. Knitting also offers the perfect opportunity to pray and meditate which contributes to my love of this pursuit. What would we do in the long winters if we were deprived of spinning, weaving and knitting? The men think it is "women's work" and we don't dare tell them how much we love it all for fear they would take it over!

Well that's enough fun for now, I need to get to the kitchen and that marvelous big cast iron woodstove which I now cannot do without! The inventor of this marvelous new creation would be totally smothered with hugs and kisses from every woman if he were ever to surface. I'll never be able to go back to cooking in my home and resort to being a fireplace dweller once again, although I've learned in this world one must be adaptable to survive.

As I knead the dough for tonight's biscuits I am surprised to find myself singing a hymn from last Sunday's Mass. Music had largely left my life since Pierre disappeared, and with him my cause for joy.

Sister Bresolle hesitantly interrupts my loud joyous refrain and I could tell by her solemn expression that something is terribly wrong. I rinse my hands and brush the flour from my face to join her. She takes me by the hand and leads me to our gathering room where I see Lambert and Father Souart waiting. They insist that we all sit down as Lambert proceeds to gently break the news that Pierre's body has been found. My heart sinks, and then he adds the horrific fact that he was decapitated. I suddenly can no longer hear their voices, everything goes black and I faint where I sit.

As I awake their tear stained faces slowly come into view. Sister Bresolle brings me a glass of cold water and tells me to drink it slowly. I ask, "Did I hear you correctly, Lambert, was my beloved Pierre found without his head?" Lambert replied, "Yes, it was nowhere to be found." My mind flashes back to the Battle of Long Sault when a few of our warriors decided to decapitate the Iroquois chief's head and display it on the top of their fort. Did my Pierre pay for that ill-conceived atrocity? Never in my worst nightmares of how they might find him did this possibility cross my mind! I asked Lambert, "Do you think this was in retribution for their chief's decapitation at Long Sault?" he replied, "This is very possible because this is the first incidence of this brutality inflicted on any of our men. Maybe they recognized his stature in our community and equated him with their chief. I can't begin to express how bereft Élizabeth and I feel at your loss and ours. In spite of the fact that he has been gone for three months, this has hit us like a deep fresh wound all over again."

# CHAPTER 32   SAYING GOODBYE

Brutus pulls the funeral wagon carrying his master's body which lies in its coffin covered with our revered flag "The Fleur de Lou" along the well-worn path leading from the fort to Notre-Dame Church. He is led along by Lieutenant Major Lambert Closse walking slowly by his side. I follow right behind flanked by Jeanne Mance and Élizabeth gently holding me up. Renée and Cousin Jean lead the entire contingent of troops resplendent in their "Montréal Blue" wool coats over their best clothes since uniforms have not been assigned to our men yet. The entire town falls in behind them in an overwhelming outpouring of love and respect for the man who meant so very much to each and every one of them. I know that there is no way all of them can fit into our small church and I fret about how they will be able to participate in the Requiem Mass with us.

Luckily it's a bright clear morning, the twenty-eighth of June and Father Souart leaves the double church doors open wide so the mourners can catch a glimpse and sing along with us to the accompaniment of trumpet, violin and drum. Six pallbearers, chosen by Lambert from so many soldiers, carry Pierre's body to the front of the sanctuary. Father blesses his coffin with Holy Water all around while praying the prescribed words of blessing in Latin. He then begins the Requiem Mass while we all sing the most solemn

123

hymns with great feeling in full voice. At the close of the Mass Father delivers a beautiful eulogy from his heart of how Pierre's profound love for his fellow man, attested to by this enormous turnout for his sending off, has been our joy. Pierre epitomized Jesus' command to love thy neighbor. The loss of this humble man will resonate in us for many years to come. He went on to say "I am honored to have known him." At this point the mourners are openly weeping right along with me as Father is unable to continue.

It is time to proceed to the church graveyard for the burial. The pallbearers carrying Pierre lead the way once again as we process slowly behind them to the spot I chose under the sprawling arms of the large oak tree, a location I thought Pierre might have chosen for himself. I know that he is pleased by the honor because I've felt his presence mightily right next to me all day long. I know he is in Paradise with Mama and Papa and his parents, and yet he can still be here with me. I feel Heaven cannot be so very far away from this earthly realm, this valley of tears.

Father performs the brief burial ceremony and once again blesses his casket with Holy Water. Then the soldiers lift off the flag (a white field with three gold fleur-de-lis) from it and fold it neatly. Lambert then presents it to me to keep and cherish until such time I give it to our child. It represents the complete sacrifice his father willingly made for his beloved country.

I kneel down beside the simple pine box, say a prayer for strength and kiss the warm wood before it is lifted and lowered into its final resting place. Then everyone, except me, scoops up a handful of soil and drops it on top of it. This is a strange tradition I have never understood and actually find repulsive and quite disrespectful to the deceased.

A very expansive buffet dinner prepared by all the women of the parish awaits us on the church grounds in the shade of the oak grove. I really need to sit down as the strain of this day is bearing down hard on me. We delayed the funeral six whole days after Pierre was found so that everyone could be contacted and hopefully this would give me time to adjust to the shock. I have found it very difficult to sleep with nightmarish possible scenarios of Pierre's last moments on this earth spinning round and round in my head.

Élizabeth places Jeanne-Cecile in my lap to dispel that glazed expression on my face. The baby kisses me on one cheek and nuzzles her ever present dolly to the other. My goodness, if a child can't help mend your broken heart, you're beyond help. Even funerals are festive in New France due to the wonderful fact that babies and children outnumber their parents by a large margin. Only four months to go before our child is born and I just can't wait to join the ranks of proud mothers. I hope this delightful thought will get me through the lonely months that lie ahead.

Renée brings me a heaping plate of food and reminds me that I must eat for the good of the baby. Everything looks so delicious and since the baby remains my prime concern I give in to all their entreaties to "Manger, manger!" I look up from my plate multiple times to talk with each friend that brings their condolences. I hope I was able to convey just how much their outpouring of love for Pierre and me has meant. I will never forget this day for all the days of my life.

I can see that the men have begun to get concerned that they've left their homes unguarded for too long. The Iroquois may have noticed that we have gathered en masse for something extraordinary so we better head for home. The ladies have begun to clean up and load the wagons with leftovers and crockery for the ride home.

Élizabeth takes me aside to invite me to come for another visit while Jeanne-Cecile starts to cry softly tugging my skirt. How could I disappoint that sweet little angel? Of course I'll come.

# CHAPTER 33   PICKING UP THE PIECES

After a consoling hiatus of two weeks, one week with Élizabeth, and not to be outdone, Renée and Jean insisted I visit them also, I feel raring to get back to my chief chef's duties at the Hotel-Dieu. All the sisters spare no special treats for my first meal back. How dear they are to me, I am especially so grateful for all their prayers that have led me out of an endless dark tunnel into the light. I will try to begin to repay them with my best efforts in the kitchen at the hottest time of the year. I am certainly extra warm this year with my sweet little one growing larger everyday within me.

All the residents greet me as if I've come back from war, which in a way, I think I have battled with demons who were determined to shake my faith at my very weakest point, the nadir of my grief. The nightmares have let up with Heaven's help, hopefully never to return.

How wonderful to dive into the flour with gusto getting dusted all over in the process. Baking is particularly satisfying for the creative streak in me. There is nothing that compares to retrieving piping hot loaves from the oven that fill the nostrils with the most heavenly aroma.

As I serve my eager loved ones I think they can see that I'm doing much better and they ask me very few questions. Sister may have gotten to them first with the request to keep our conversation light and they should show extra appreciation for the dinner instead. Of course I enquire how each of them have fared without me and just how are they doing? Most elderly folks love the summer because they can finally thaw out, although it's amazing how some of them even wear sweaters on this hot mid-July day! Hot soup is a perennial favorite with them, as it is with me since the preparation is so simple. My soup is packed with so many fresh vegetables harvested this morning from our own garden it really resembles a hearty stew.

There is one interesting phenomenon developing that really isn't all that surprising, suddenly the folks are entertaining many more visitors than usual. It seems that every unattached gentleman in town has found an excuse to come and visit and hopefully make a good impression on me. Subtlety is no bachelor's strong suit and they well know that Pierre departed only four months ago and was buried less than a month ago. These men are not the least bit timid or lacking in testosterone.

As for me, I'm not really in the least bit ready for another love to enter my life, but as Élizabeth and Renée have both pointed out my baby is entering this world in three months' time without a father and I really can't stay in the hospital forever. This is no place to raise a child but I can't go back to our home alone. It's just not safe for a woman to live alone without a man, so I really don't have the luxury of taking my time. I'm a romantic at heart, but my situation is beyond extraordinary and calls for a much more practical approach. There certainly must be an excellent man among all these that will be a good father and husband.

When I think about it, any man who is confident enough to marry me with my hard luck life story and a baby on the way has to be a very special man indeed. We shall see what happens next through the grace of God and probably a nudge in the right direction from Father and the Sisters. They have never been known to shy away from their roles as matchmakers for our town, and every suggestion is welcome. I'm all of eighteen and one half and looking for husband number three, am I not a matchmaker's delight!?

## CHAPTER 34   THE SEARCH IS ON

There is a matchmaker par excellence in town whom I consulted about my decision to marry Pierre just last year. This time I don't have any candidate in mind for her approval so I am totally open to any help she can give me. Marguerite Bourgeoys (our town's living saint) welcomes me with open arms although she profoundly regrets that the mission I am on is necessary. She has been thinking and praying about my situation and has been expecting to see me to discuss it. She agrees that one criteria narrows down our options, there can be no more soldiers or men with jobs within or for the fort. The danger quotient must be reduced, although it will never be eliminated living here. Marguerite can't wait to share this with me.

"I have just heard some great news straight from Governor d'Avaugour I am thrilled to tell you. He is planning to send Captain Pierre Boucher of Trois-Rivières to France to see the King to request three thousand French Regular troops to come and defend our colony!" I exclaim "How wonderful, even if we receive just one thousand men our troubles will be greatly lessened and all of us can begin to breathe a little easier!"

"Getting back to the issue at hand, I think I have the perfect match for you. This is Honoré Langlois dit Lachapelle et Croustille's story: Ten years ago he was a soldier of King Louis XIV when he left Paris accompanied by Paul Lauzon on one of three ships headed to Québec. This was two years before I arrived with the Grande Recrue in the summer of 1651. A few months later Governor Maisonneuve arrived back from France where he had beseeched the King for soldiers to help defend Ville-Marie and made a stop in Québec City where Paul Lauzon granted him a reinforcement of ten men including Honoré. He is a hat maker, a trade he learned from his father. He has never married, although he has told me that at thirty years of age he is more than ready to marry and start a family. His given name, Honoré, is a very auspicious name meaning 'to honor a wish or promise'. If you were to marry him, I can tell you one thing for sure, your family will always have food on the table because he is an avid hunter who has made sure our larder has remained well stocked with fish and game throughout these many years, all at no cost to us! He is a most kind and generous man who I'm sure you'll find possesses a terrific sense of humor."

This is an intriguing idea and if I'm not mistaken he has yet to appear at the hospital as a "sudden visitor." I know who he is from Church where he is always alone. I just assumed he was a confirmed bachelor.

"Marguerite, please let him know that I'd love to have him come to Sunday dinner this week so we can get acquainted. They say that the best route to a man's heart is through his stomach and I have an advantage there for I'm an excellent cook."

"I'm still unsure if he'd be willing to take on a woman who will very soon be a new mother. If he is interested, despite this complication and my history in general, I'm definitely anxious to meet such a confident man!"

The week passed quickly while I consulted with Jeanne, Father Souart and all the sisters in residence. Everyone agreed with Marguerite's choice for my third husband, and with God's help my forever mate. I value their opinions so very much. Of course I've prayed to Jesus to send me a sign if Honoré is the one. I will await His answer which I've learned by experience could come in the most unexpected way. I've also prayed to Pierre, but I already know how important it was to him that I not be left alone, so much so that he hesitated to marry me in the first place.

It's time to pick some fresh vegetables from our bountiful garden for supper. As I bend down to pull some carrots I'm suddenly surrounded by dozens of blue butterflies. I dare not move a muscle to hasten their departure. They encircle me, and then as if on cue take off into the blue sky, back to heaven from whence they came as the sign of my Lord's approval. Through grateful tears I say "Thank you Jesus, Mother Mary, Pierre, Mama and Papa! I have received your message loud and clear!" It's full speed ahead for me and my sweet little one who delights in awakening me at night with her acrobatics.

I think it's a little girl whom I will name Marie in honor of Our Lady and myself as per our French tradition. Of course if it's a boy, Pierre for his father will be his name. I waddle back to the kitchen with as light a step as I can manage toting my basket full of vegetables singing as I go.

I'm anxious to relate my butterfly story to whomever will listen. While I have their attention, I inquire, of all the dishes I make, what is their favorite? The consensus is my meat pie is the very best along with my fruit pies. That is probably the best meal for a bachelor since I very much doubt he'd ever bother to make that for himself.

This Sunday dawns warm, bright and beautiful. I hurry to get home from Mass because I still need to prepare some of the side dishes for us all. Jeanne insists that she will assist me with the meal for everyone else, so that Honoré and I can have a quiet meal alone afterwards to get to know each other. I gratefully accept the help since for some reason I'm a bit flustered over the whole prospect of today's meeting.

There is a knock at the back door and I rush to dust off flour from my face and apron. I open the door and am surprised to find Honoré smiling from ear to ear, his large dark brown eyes twinkling, holding a big bouquet of fresh wild flowers in his left hand and a string of ten dressed rabbits dangling from his right. He makes such a humorous picture that we both break out in hearty laughter. I try to compose myself and choose to take the flowers. I declare, "Welcome Monsieur Langlois dit Lachapelle et Croustille. I was expecting you to arrive by the front door. I'm Marie Pontonnier, your chef for dinner this afternoon," sounding as formal as I could muster. "Please call me Honoré, Madame Pontonnier, thank you so much for your kind invitation." Honoré proceeds to bow low while holding high the rabbits so they would not hit the floor. Our laughter begins once again. Oh, I do believe we will get along splendidly, for I really need a man that can keep me laughing right now.

We spent a lovely time, with me serving one dish after another and him complementing me on each one saying it was the very best he'd ever tasted. How this man hasn't been snatched up a long time ago is beyond me. The answer is simple mathematics, I tend to forget that there are so many more men than ladies on this island. That has to be the reason for he is a quite handsome and strong Frenchman perhaps five feet nine inches tall. Most of our men become muscular from clearing the land to build our farms and homes and therefore at mealtime possess ravenous appetites from all the hard work in the fresh air.

In between mouthfuls he puts forward his case as to why he would be a good husband and father, even going so far as to promise to adopt my child and raise it as his own. Oh my goodness, maybe he really does like my cooking!

The next weeks flew by as we bonded over a few more meat and various berry pies. We decide to make our decision official with a marriage contract to be signed on October sixteenth, 1661, which is only three weeks before my due date of November eighth. We are cutting it close but that seems to be how my life is working out. We've decided to keep the celebration to a few very close friends since our wedding date hopefully will be December fifth, a month after the baby will arrive which is a month before I turn nineteen. Father Souart will apply for a special dispensation from the Church for us to marry during Advent which he assures us will not be a problem because of our special circumstances.

I can't wait for this winter when this hectic pace will slow and we can settle down to a more normal life, forming our new little family of three. I will finally become the mother which I have so long envisioned that I will be.

## CHAPTER 35   BACK TO NOTARY BÉNIGNE BASSET'S OFFICE

Honoré takes my hand tenderly and gently tilts my head so that our brown eyes meet. "Marie are you sure you are ready to sign our marriage contract? Am I rushing you along in my ardent desire to take you as my wife?" Through tears that have just now formed in response to his sweet entreaty I nod and declare "Yes, I'm very sure that we can build a happy life together. You have waited a very long time for the right woman to come along! I hope that I can fill that role for you and make a happy home for the three of us." I have managed to cause him to tear up with tears of relief and happiness. He squeezes my hand and off we go to the Notary Basset's office to make our pledges official.

As we enter we are both shocked that the room is packed with well-wishers. Jeanne Mance is smiling ear to ear thrilled that she was able to gather so many friends to witness our signing of the document and to add their signatures, some of them with great flourishes. Our noisy jolly group departs and heads over to the gathering room at the hospital where tea and pies await.

The dear sisters, Father Souart and the patients comprising the other members of my family are able to join in the festivities. Father leads us in saying grace and then adds a fervent prayer. "May our dear Lord

136

bless you both with a very long and happy life made rich by many children." Everyone joined in a resounding "AMEN!"

Just three weeks later on November ninth, I was awakened in the middle of the night by painful contractions. I arose and woke up Jeanne with, "She is on her way right on schedule. I'm so sorry I have to wake you up!" The call went out and soon all the sisters surrounded me in my little room. Two of them had experienced deliveries before so I tried to relax which is so much easier said than done. I was so tense and fearful which I suppose is understandable even though I knew in every fiber of my being that this little one is strong and will be just fine. Anytime you are going through something so foreign to you which you've only seen others go through, it is completely different when it is happening to you. I couldn't stop shaking despite all the dear nuns rubbing my brow, taking turns holding my hand and reminding me to breathe. I concentrated on the crucifix on the wall and prayed to Jesus with all my strength for strength.

The hours passed when at daybreak Honoré arrived having had a premonition that little Marie was on her way. Jeanne insisted that he remain in the kitchen, have something to eat and keep the cook company while he frets and paces.

Meanwhile my water finally broke which pleased the sisters who were all relieved since they said it would hasten my contractions and ease delivery. From my perspective the pain intensified considerably and my cries increased in volume. The entire hospital must know at this point how I'm doing!

"It's time to push, Marie! I see her head so it won't be long now". I pushed with all my rapidly waning power because the next words I long to hear is "She's here!" "Good job Marie, little Marie has made her entrance!" The baby cried out her greeting mightily for all to hear. Honoré heard the news first from Jeanne since he was just on the other side of the door unable to follow her command to stay in the kitchen. "It's a girl Honoré, and they are both doing fine! Marie is very anxious that little Marie be baptized right away. Since Father Souart has just come on his rounds, maybe you, Father, the Godfather and I could bring little Marie right over to Notre Dame Church. We are so lucky that it is unseasonably warm and sunny today. Otherwise I would insist that she be baptized right here. You better go fetch whomever you've decided to honor as Godfather. The baby will be ready when you return and you may see her and Marie then. She needs to get some rest."

The new father was off on his mission in a flash thrilled to finally have a job to do and propelled by the prospect of seeing both Maries on his return.

Honoré came bounding back to rejoin the group with his dear friend and fellow merchant Charles Le Moyne. Jeanne held the little one, all wrapped up warmly for her first breath of fresh air. Honoré admired her but was content to let Jeanne carry the sweet little sleeping angel nestled in her basket.

Father led the way to the church, through the door to the baptismal font, located just inside the door. He lit the blessed beeswax candle. Jeanne as Godmother held little Marie's tiny head over the Holy Water. The little one barely whimpered as Father poured the water over her brow and dark brown hair saying in Latin "I baptize thee in the name of the Father and of the Son and of the Holy Spirit." He then pronounced her a Christian and member of the Holy Roman Catholic Apostolic Church. Father had prepared a baptismal certificate which he dated and signed, had the Godparents sign and presented it to Honoré. He then recorded in the parish register her name Marie Martin, her mother's name, Marie Pontonnier and her father's name Pierre Martin posthumously. Honoré vowed to himself that he would adopt and raise her as his first child but he realized that she would always retain her baptismal name of Marie Martin.

Honoré thanked Father and mentioned, "I'm sure you know how anxious I am to get back to Marie and see how she is doing. I haven't seen her yet today!" "Of course you must be. May God bless you all! Please pass on my blessing and good wishes to Marie. I pray she recovers quickly for in less than a month you both will be back here pronouncing your marriage vows!"

# CHAPTER 36   THE WEDDING GIFT

"Where in the world are we headed, Honoré? We aren't going to spend our first night together in the barn are we? I wouldn't mind it but it is much too cold for the baby! Oh my heavens, you've built us a new home directly behind your old one!"

"Yes sweetheart, it just dawned on me the day we met that I should bring my bride to a brand new home for our brand new life! We would need a much larger one for all the children we plan to have, and why not build it behind my existing workshop and little home. There is plenty of land back here to accommodate it and the garden. That way it is a very short trip home for dinner!"

"No wonder you've been famished every time you came for supper. I just can't believe you've been able to build an entire house in such a short time. It's an amazing feat!"

"Well, I've had a great deal of help from many good friends. I am very surprised that it's remained a secret from you. I thought surely someone would slip up. You really had no idea, Marie? Not the slightest hint from anyone?"

"Not one iota, now let's go in for a tour of our new house! We need to start a fire in that new fireplace so I can nurse our little one." My amazing husband is beaming, he sweeps open the door and carries both of us to the big rocking chair seating us ever so gently before the fire. For he had thought of everything and had asked Jean to slip out of the reception to go light the fire so that the whole house would be warm and glowing for his girls. He gives us both a sweet kiss upon our foreheads and then leaves us alone to enjoy the indescribable miracle that God has devised for His babies to continue to grow and thrive on their mothers' nourishment.

Our little Marie is all that I expected and so very much more. This delicate little one, the answer to all my longings, is perfect in every way. Her cry is almost apologetic as if she hates to interrupt my pursuits but she needs me for a minute or so. Honoré is totally enraptured with her and I usually find him gazing down transfixed with a smile of total love upon his face. Thank you, thank you sweet Jesus for all the blessings you've bestowed upon us especially for your choice of Honoré for us. The dear man will have to wait awhile for the consummation of our marriage because it hasn't even been a month since I gave birth. Marie will be one month old in three days. Honoré has assured me that he is a very patient man and I should not give it a second thought. We have our whole lives ahead of us which he is sure will be a very long time. We want the exact same things in life, many children over many fruitful blissful years.

Little Marie has nursed herself to sleep so I place her in her cozy basket. I have almost fallen asleep as well in my reverie so I decide to join Honoré

141

in our fluffy feather bed where I find him sleeping peacefully with a contented smile upon his countenance. All review of our lovely wedding day can certainly wait for tomorrow or maybe he'll awake for the 2:00 am feeding although somehow I seriously doubt it.

Our new house awakens at dawn, the baby for breakfast, Honoré to milk the cow, feed the chickens and his hard working dark brown stallion named Rex. He is smiling a sly smile when he enters the back door. "Marie, I have another surprise for you!" "You must be kidding, Honoré. I haven't gotten you even one gift, I feel terrible!" "Not to worry my love, come and see." I slip on my favorite old blue sweater and take his hand as he guides me to the barn not knowing what could possibly await me. And there to my utter amazement is Grace, my sweet confidante horse and my trusty Grande Pyrénées Brigitte who almost knocks me down in her enthusiastic greeting.

"Honoré, how in the world did you arrange this?" "Well, Pierre remembered that he had promised you when you left that when you were able to accommodate them you should have your horse and dog back. I agreed that I would love to make them part of our growing family. I'll need to buy some more sheep for Brigitte to herd and keep guard over. I hear she is happiest when she has a job to do. I'm famished, let's get in and eat our first meal together in our new home."

# CHAPTER 37   HAPPINESS TURNS TO HORROR

The Christmas Reveillion and New Year's Eve holidays were a blur of glee with visitors coming and going anxious to behold our beautiful little Marie. She has her father Pierre's big blue eyes and my thick wavy dark brown hair which I gathered up onto the top of her head and crowned with a satin bow. She has charmed the town with her sweet smile and sunny disposition.

On New Year's morn I opened my eyes to find Honoré smiling down at me. He proceeded to retrieve from under the bed a scroll tied with a red satin ribbon. I unrolled it to find the official adoption papers signed in very large letters with a flourish–Honoré Langlois dit La Chapelle et Croustille. Once again he proved true to his name of Honoré. I could not hold back the tears that flowed in happy gratitude and neither could he. Little Marie chimed in, of course not knowing what had just transpired, but very sure her little tummy was empty.

The month of January passed in quiet domesticity, a reflection of the soft snow that fell silently on our bucolic village.

The town's peace was shattered by gunfire on Monday morning, February sixth, 1662. While Simon Roy and his friends were cutting trees a band of marauding Iroquois who were camped near Montréal attacked them with arrows and guns. Governor Maisonneuve immediately sent his servants Pierre Pigeon and William Fleming to summon Sergeant- Major Lambert Closse and twelve of his men at the fort. They rushed to find Simon and two friends laying bleeding in the snow, shot through with arrows. The Iroquois then concentrated their fire on Lambert Closse and his soldiers. A long battle ensued in which the Sergeant-Major Closse's pistol jammed and he fell mortally wounded next to his trusty dog Pilote who tried in vain to rally him. The remaining soldiers and townsfolk who came running to assist were able to force the Iroquois to retreat, to return another day. We lost Sergeant-Major Lambert Closse, four of our soldiers, Simon Roy and two of his friends.

Honoré felt torn between his desire to help them and his love and responsibility to guard the baby and me. I was understandably very relieved that he remained at home with us.

The week of mourning that followed was excruciating. My best friend Élizabeth Moyen was married to Lambert Closse in a double wedding with Pierre Gadois and me. She lost both of her parents and her home in an Iroquois massacre as a youth, she lost her first baby, and now she must endure the crushing loss of her Warrior Hero husband to the brutal Onotagues Iroquois. Her precious little daughter Jeanne-Cecile, who when my Pierre was missing such a short time ago, had tried to console me with her little rag doll, has now lost her beloved Da-Da.

We mourn with so many families. Jeanne Godard, a very dear friend who gave birth to her first child, a baby boy named Jean last May has lost her dear Simon whom she married only three years ago. We have been friends since she was good enough to testify for me against René Besnard Bourjoly at his witchcraft trial.

We pray that we can hold out in Ville-Marie until the King's soldiers arrive this summer. Of course none of us is sure that King Louis the XIV will have mercy on us and send us troops. The Iroquois will be a constant worry until then. They realize that they have killed our Sergeant-Major and are rejoicing at their prowess, but we know they won't remain content for long. Dear Lord have mercy on us and please preserve us from another massacre. Mother Mary remember the tiny village named Ville-Marie in your honor.

Father Gabriel Souart was completely overwhelmed with consoling all the families and asked if they would mind if he had one Requiem Funeral for all of their fallen loved ones at the same time. Since the ground is frozen solid, their burials would have to wait until late May at which time he would preside at another Mass and they would be buried with full Military Honors here in the sacred ground of Notre Dame Cemetery. Everyone was amenable to that arrangement and in their shock said not a word in protest.

145

Father Souart's face mirrored all of our grief as if he absorbed as much as he could and had reached his absolute limit. We all tend to think of our Pastors as superhuman with endless capacity to handle every crisis. Times like these show their humanity and frailty, their utter loneliness. Dearest Jesus, please hold up our beloved Father Souart, for I'm afraid he won't be able to bear up under this strain.

We didn't have to wait for long for another attack. On June twenty-seventh Michel Louvard dit Desjardins, who was the husband of Francoise-Jacqueline Nadreau was killed by the Wolf Indians on his very own doorstep. It was determined that the perpetrators were drunk, so on the very next day an ordinance was passed forbidding anyone from "selling intoxicating beverages to the Savages, given the assassination of the said Desjardins, committed the previous night by drunken Savages." *

*Auger, Grande Recrue, p.83. Quoted from the Documents Judiciares of the Archives Judiciares de Montreal.

# CHAPTER 38   HOPES FOR RELIEF DASHED

We received no troops in the summer of 1662 to everyone's great dismay. The summer of 1663 again held the promise of troops from France but instead King Louis XIV threw a title at the ongoing problem. We are now a "Royal Province" which is all well and good but still a crushing blow to our hopes for a less stressful life.

The King is now campaigning throughout France for women to join us with the odd title of "Filles du Roi" which translates to "Daughters of the King". He is trying to entice willing young women with the promise of a dowry and proper clothes crowned with a lovely bonnet for each. I hear they are even searching orphanages to find girls who will jump at the chance for a better life in the New World. I wonder how many of them will depart those awful ships at the first port in France when they realize just what they have gotten themselves into.

Not everyone is cut from the rugged cloth that we women were who came here ten years ago with only empty pockets, complete faith in our Lord and hope in our hearts. I really don't begrudge the King's plan for generous enticements but I do feel he is being very irresponsible to send them here without the proper protection of soldiers to keep them and all of us safer from Iroquois incursions. Why send more defenseless young women to join us without commensurate protection? We do still have a "six men to one woman" ratio and I understand his desire to even that out a bit so the birthrate will rise. We are just bitterly disappointed that our pleas for troops seems to have fallen on deaf ears. Our only recourse is to pray, pray, pray for our King to change his mind. Our Lord, the King of my heart is always listening to us, but sometimes it is very difficult to construe His plans.

On a much happier note, Honoré and I are expecting our first baby in January 1664. We are both very excited to say the least. Honoré is walking on air at the prospect of the possibility that I'm bearing his first son. Of course he always adds the words, "Boy or girl, dearest Lord, may the baby be healthy!" Our little Marie will be two years old on November ninth. I'm so glad she will have a brother or sister to grow up with, but this time I'm not at all certain whether it's a boy or a girl.

Now as the prospect of our expanding family looms Honoré is fretting over his income being adequate to provide for us. I've reminded him often how God always provides for his children, yet he is determined to add another job to his duties. Since we are so short on troops for security, the men of the village have come up with a solution in discussions with the Governor. He has agreed to choose a police force from willing candidates. Needless to say I'm really not happy at this prospect of Honoré being one of those candidates. There is no way that I won't be worried every moment that he is on duty. It's bad enough for me now when he goes out hunting the woods for our food. I can't help visualizing an Iroquois lying in wait behind every tree! I pray he changes his mind about applying as a candidate next spring. After our baby is born his work load will increase tremendously around our home since I'll be nursing a little one once again. Please Lord, I pray that every one of our residents need new hats soon, so he will be busy all winter and will forget this crazy notion of joining the new police force.

On January sixteenth our bright red and rosy addition announced her arrival with a loud cry as she entered the cold of a Montréal morn. Her new father can wait no longer and blasts into the birthing room toting Little Marie.

"Oh, Honoré, are you terribly disappointed? I know how very much you wanted a boy."

"Now how could I be the least bit disappointed when I look down at this gorgeous little one! She will be the perfect companion to our Little Marie. Marie, how do you like your little sister?" She nods and smiles a broad grin in approval, her eyes opened wide.

"Can't you just picture the two of them playing with their little dolls? I need to make another one soon for our little Jeanne. I thought I'd like to name her Jeanne for your Dad, Jean, and I'm sure my mentor Jeanne Mance will be thrilled with the honor as well.

149

What do you think, does she look like a Jeanne to you?"

"Absolutely, and I'm so touched that you would honor my father. I know he appreciates it as well and is smiling down on us from above as we speak."

"I know, I'm so glad you feel that way. I also know that my mother really wasn't fond of her name, Felicité, so she won't mind."

Our typically frigid winter has passed in peaceful contentment for our little family of four. We are so anxious to breathe in the fresh air of spring. I am not at all anxious to broach the sensitive topic of the new police department but it is right around the corner so I have to break our silence on the topic.

"Honoré, do you still want to proffer your name for police officer?"

"Yes, absolutely, I feel it is my duty. I'm an excellent shot and I feel it is my obligation to do my part."

"But you have already served over ten years for France as a soldier. Isn't that more than enough?"

"I know, but I feel that I must at least try. I've heard there are quite a few men coming forward."

"Well, you know where I stand on this and if you feel you must, I will not stand in your way. You make the final decisions in our home and it is my obligation as a good wife to stand by you."

"Thank you, Marie."

There were sixteen men who offered their names to the Governor and he took seven days to pick five men among them. I breathed a very deep sigh of relief when Honoré wasn't chosen and I noticed one thing they all had in common. They were all men without wives and children. God bless our Governor for realizing that was the most judicious course to take. I'm sure many women across the village are as thrilled as I that their husbands will not be police officers.

# CHAPTER 39   SUMMER OF 1665 BRINGS GOOD NEWS FOR ALL

The King is sending our long awaited troops, twelve hundred strong, over June, July, August and September! We are so thrilled that our Lord and the King have had mercy on us. They are French Regular troops from the Carigines-Salieres Regiment. They will be assigned all over New France with special attention to our beleaguered Montréal because the carnage has proven to be greatest in our tiny Ville-Marie.

The entire summer should be taken up with celebrations at the docks as they arrive to an exceptionally warm reception. More "Daughters of the King" will be arriving simultaneously on the same ships. Many have had their eyes on certain soldiers and vice versa so we expect Father Souart will be extremely busy performing marriage ceremonies this summer which will add to the gaiety.

As for us we are happily ensconced in our new home with our beautiful little ones running to and fro. They love to join me in the vegetable patch and to scurry among the chickens. Marie is three and a half and Jeanne is eighteen months, and they are the best of friends and may it always be so.

I have a big surprise for Honoré at dinner this noon which I hope delights him. He seems to be in an extraordinarily good mood so I will take advantage of that, plus I've made him his favorite foods. As we sit down to partake he says, "Alright Marie, I've been smelling your fabulous meat pie all morning wafting through the window of the workshop so what do you have to tell me?"

"Well, Honoré, I'm very sure I'm with child again."

"Sweetheart, I wondered when you would tell me. I figured that out a few weeks ago! Did you think I would be anything but delighted? I thought you knew me better than that."

"Well, I hesitated since last time your reaction was so frantic that you felt you needed to join the police force to make more money. I guess I was afraid what you'd decide to do this time!"

"Not to worry, my love, I'm sure the influx of soldiers and young ladies will keep me very busy. I hear our new Intendant, Jean Talon wants us to experiment with raising barley and hops for beer. So I'm thinking of planting some of our acreage with these new crops. What do you think about that idea?"

"So you've been thinking about all this for some time? You are a constant surprise to me although I guess I'm an open book to you!"

"I hope in the future you will never hesitate to talk to me about anything, good news or bad. I'm thrilled that we are expecting again. When do you figure the day will be?"

"It looks like during the holidays either Christmas or New Year's should be the due date."

"Wonderful, a precious gift from our dear Lord for the most joyful time of the year! Now come over here so I can give you a proper hug and kiss."

As usual I worry about things that never come about, things that are all in Your hands, my Sweet Jesus. I am very glad that another dear child is on the way and I thank You so much!

Our colony is also getting a new form of government this year called a Sovereign Council. The Council is appointed by the King and his representative, Jean-Baptiste Colbert. It is made up of three people: the Governor, the Intendant and the Bishop. These are presently: Governor Chevalier de Mezy, Intendant Jean Talon and Bishop Francois de Laval. We will pray that they can work together for the mutual good of our entire colony. I'm sure there will be a period of adjustment to this new system of government for everyone, so we shall see how this will work out going forward.

This is shaping up to be a banner year for us all. The harvest was excellent and was quite a big job preserving for the winter. I find I'm really slowing down as I near the holidays. I want to decorate with my usual enthusiasm but with taking care of two little ones, with all the attendant duties of the farm and my rapidly expanding girth, I'm exhausted. I find there is only so much that one person can accomplish in a day and must be satisfied with less. This soon to arrive little one will have to be content with the outgrown clothes of Marie and Jeanne since I've not picked up my knitting for months.

My restless sleep of December thirtieth culminated in the arrival of our third child. Honoré was his usual exuberant self while announcing the birth. "Heaven be praised for we have our son!" I insist that he be named for him for many reasons, Honoré is a fine name, that I'm sure he will live up to as has his father.

# CHAPTER 40   SUDDEN DARKNESS

Both of our hearts were pierced through with unimaginable sorrow when our little angel, Honoré, failed to awaken February eighteenth, 1666. He was only seven weeks old and showed no signs of any illness when I nursed him for the last time at two in the morning.

Thank God we have our little girls who console us tremendously, but they do not understand either why Jesus needed to take him to Heaven. We find it very, very difficult to say as Job did "The Lord giveth and the Lord hath taken away, blessed be the Name of the Lord," (Job 1:21) for His ways are inscrutable to us mortals.

With the coming of the warmth of summer I realized that I was expecting once more. This time I had to tell Honoré right away because he has taken the loss of his son so hard. He reacted just as I suspected he would by lifting me off the floor and spinning me round and round. Each of the girls wanted their Papa to spin them around just as he did Mama. Soon we were all laughing heartily, for Honoré and me it was probably the first time since that dark February morn.

There will be no more looking back since it would not be good for the baby or any of us. This summer in Montréal we are feeling as if we can finally breathe. The difference the King's troops have made is truly palpable. There have been a few skirmishes on the outskirts of town but we have not lost any soldiers or additional residents. I feel like saluting every one of those shining soldiers when we meet for it's because of them that I can relax a bit when Honoré goes out hunting. He repeatedly assures me that he is still on guard because the Iroquois are a cunning enemy who can never be taken lightly and the troops cannot be expected to cover every inch of territory. Of course I realize this, but would prefer to believe and hope that we may sign a treaty soon and be able to live in peace.

Exactly one year ago almost to the day that we lost our sweet Honoré, I gave birth to another girl on February twenty-fifth, 1667. I named her Marguerite in honor of my dear chaperone who died aboard ship on my voyage to Ville-Marie some eleven years ago and for my dear friend Marguerite Bourgeoys, our town's living saint. Our little Marguerite is a blessing from above. We will never forget our little Honoré but she has helped to ease our grief over him and has won a unique place in our hearts.

Our colony's Intendant, Jean Talon, has ordered the first census of New France to be taken up this summer of '67. Our listing reads as follows: Honoré, 35 years old, Marie Pontonnier, his wife, 24 years old. Marie 6, Jeanne 4, Marguerite 3 months. Two cattle, 20 acres under cultivation. Neighbors, Gillen Sanson (Lauzon) and Pierre Chauvin. There were found to be

668 families and 3,215 souls in New France as of June 1667.

All of New France rejoiced exceedingly when we finally signed a peace treaty with the Iroquois League. Our church bells pealed on and on in raucous celebration as we gathered on the church grounds for a grand picnic. Oh how we pray that this time the Iroquois will adhere to the terms of the treaty, one of which is that they must return all captured French. The following is the amazing story of one of them.

"In 1660, nine-year-old Anne Baillargeon at Trois-Rivières was captured by the Iroquois and spent seven years in captivity, adopting the customs and lifestyle of the natives. When Prouville de Tracy ordered the Iroquois to release all of their captives in 1667, Anne decided to remain with the Amerindians and ran off into the forest. There, she claims that the apparition of a nun appeared to her and threatened to punish her if she did not return to her people. When she was brought back to Québec, Monsieur de Tracy placed her in the Ursuline school, where she had been for one month in 1660 prior to her capture. There, she recognized the portrait of the recently-deceased Mother Marie de Sainte-Joseph as the nun who had appeared to her in the forest". *

Her parents, Marie Metayer and Mathurin Baillargeon, had never despaired of ever seeing her again. I can just imagine their joy when they were reunited.

*Peter J. Gagne, Before the King's
Daughters  The Filles à Marier, 1634-1662
p.226

# CHAPTER 41    POINTE-AUX-TREMBLES

1669 proves to be a pivotal year for us with another pregnancy for me, obvious by the end of February. For Honoré a new land beckoned to him with more acreage and a deal he just could not refuse.

Pointe-Aux-Trembles* is located on the northern portion of the Island of Montréal where the St. Lawrence and Rivières des Prairies join and was selected as a location to defend Montréal. A fort will be built in the near future. The first concession of land was given to the priests of the Seminar of St. Suplice Ville-Marie. On April 5, 1669, Mr. Quelylias gave forty acres of land to Jean Oury dit la Marche and to others with the proviso that a church and mill be built. Honoré was also granted a franchise to Pointe-Aux-Trembles and is very anxious to be fully involved in the founding of a new church and town. He realizes that this will all take time and patience and doesn't intend to move our family there until things are well established which is a great relief to me. I have very mixed feelings about the prospect of uprooting the family. I realize Pointe-Aux-Trembles is still part of Montréal but our friends are here and in much closer proximity and our church of Notre-Dame holds so many memories. The idea of a new church and a whole new town excites the pioneer spirit in Honoré but for me the whole concept is daunting. I would be very happy to remain right where we are. I guess the nesting spirit is more prominent in females especially ones who are almost continuously pregnant or nursing babies.

Our fourth beautiful baby girl arrived on September nineteenth. It had been a more difficult pregnancy this time since I had to endure a full Montréal summer at the end of my term. I am thrilled that she can get off to a good start before the full brunt of winter sets in. We named her Anne-Thérèse for no particular reason at all other than the lovely sound of it. I hear that she slept through her baptism at Notre-Dame church. St. Anne was Jesus' grandmother and St. Teresa of Avila, Spain was canonized in 1622 so our Anne-Thérèse has two patron saints to watch over and guide her.

Honoré is patiently waiting for the birth of a baby boy. He dearly loves all his little girls and gives each of them plenty of attention and affection but I know how much he'd like to be able to pass on his trade to a son as his father did. I'll do my best to give him one just as soon as our Lord decides it's time to balance the sexes in the Langlois household. I have a feeling that it won't be long before that happy day arrives.

Jesus has apparently decided to fix our colony's man to woman ratio by inspiring more and more young women to take up our King Louis XIV's offer of cash to cross the forbidding sea. The influx this year has numbered so many that it's perhaps twice as many as in previous years. Our Intendant has had to build a facility to hold them all until they can find their mates. Our notary has been overrun and can't keep up with the marriage contracts volume. At Church it is most obvious with the banns of marriage announcements every Sunday going on and on. The customary three weeks of Wedding banns has sometimes been dispensed with so the couples can get married right away. It seems that not only is our King anxious to fill our colony with children, but so are the couples very ready to run down the aisle. Double, triple and quadruple marriage ceremonies are so common I know that Father Souart is exhausted but it is a happy depletion of his stamina as opposed to the overwhelming sorrow he had to endure before our treaty with the Iroquois was signed.

I'm glad to see our population burgeon with this influx of the "King's Daughters" or the "Filles de Roi" a moniker coined by our Marguerite Bourgeoys. This name has helped a bit to dispel the girls' undeserved reputation as prostitutes which has been spread by rumor, innuendo and in print for years. These scurrilous accusations are unfounded from what I can see. No one has been accused of that crime that I know of and they have packed our church to the rafters every Sunday. Honoré foresaw this and now a new location, church and town is looking much more appealing to me.

Business for him has been very steady and I'm happy to see him so content now that he is training an apprentice to help him. He is also helping with the planting and farm duties and has proven invaluable to both of us.

In Pointe-Aux-Trembles they have established the Parish of L'Enfant Jesus and the priests have begun to celebrate Mass and administer the sacraments in the home of Francois Bau now that the population is growing. The Parish of L'Enfant Jesus was established on July 28, 1671 when Picote the Sieur de Belestre was granted the concession.

By the end of October I decided to tell Honoré one night after he snuffed out the candle and climbed into bed, "I have a secret, sweetheart."

"Well, what could that possibly be? Could it be that you are bearing a little one once again?"

"Oh, you are such a rascal, Honoré!"

"Yes, and I think you like me that way, don't you?"

"Yes, I must admit I do! What if I have a boy that is just like his father, what ever will I do with the both of you?"

"I think I'll believe it when I see it because that would be a dream come true for me! I'll seal that with a big kiss my love! Yes, now it must happen!"

"Good night sweetheart, sweet dreams!"

On June twenty-sixth, 1672 Honoré got his wish, thank you Jesus! Our little Jean Langlois was baptized and became a member of our Church hollering all the way. He had nothing to complain about on that beautiful summer day. Oh dear, maybe he will be just like his father! No, let me clarify that. Honoré is a boisterous happy story teller in a good way, and he is very rarely angry with anyone. If he ever is he doesn't let it show, but keeps it to himself and then tells me all about it. Yes, I hope Jean grows up to emulate his father who is perfect for me so I'm sure he will someday marry a wonderful woman!


*Back then Pointe-Aux-Trembles was known as Cote Saint-Jean

# CHAPTER 42   NEW LIFE

On a bright spring morning almost three years later, April 15, 1675, we had our next child.

"Honoré, it's a boy!"

"Oh, my Lord, we have another son, Marie?! I now have a hunting party of three! I can't wait to teach my boys the fine points of the hunt. Thank you, dear Lord!"

"Isn't he adorable, Honoré, do you think we should name him Andre?"

"It's a perfect name for a fine man. Yes, Andre Langlois dit La Chapelle et Croustille sounds regal."

We are now a family of eight with four lovely girls and two baby boys. Our oldest, Marie, is now fourteen years old and a wonderful help to me with the children and the cooking. I try not to put too much responsibility on her shoulders because she deserves to have a normal life like every young woman. I wish that I had grown up with brothers and sisters to love.

Pointe-Aux-Trembles has been progressing nicely and now has a flour mill, a very important feature for every town. Now it is officially "The Mission Pointe-Aux-Trembles of the Province of Québec" established as of 1674. The fort took two years to build and is now complete. The plans for the Church are well underway. The Church of L'Enfant Jesus will be built of stone and measure thirty-six by twenty-four feet which we hope will be adequate and permanent. A windmill will be built simultaneously.

I continue to dread our move when the town is sufficiently finished. Why Honoré thinks that moving our family into such a remote location ten miles away is a good idea is beyond me. The whole town's purpose is its strategic location for the defense of Montréal. I really don't relish planting ourselves on the front line of battle. "Dearest Lord, may you make it impossible for us to go. You specialize in the impossible, so I'm placing our fates in Your capable hands. Amen."

I really doubt there are enough families who will be willing to pull up roots, take the risk and relocate. The men are raring to go and the wives and mothers are all praying that we can change their minds. It's the talk of the town and causing friction between the sexes all over. The ladies feel that only the single soldiers without families should occupy the town. None of the ladies trust the Iroquois to respect the peace treaty. They have shed so much French blood that we are forever scarred, so much so that the mere mention of their name produces a feeling of sheer panic in us. Why are men so willing to take up arms and enter the fray?

Men always say that they are the ones governed by logic and we ladies are the purely emotional ones dominated by our hearts. In this case they seem to throw logic to the wind and risk far too much to prove

166

their grit. I guess we will never understand them nor will they ever fathom us. Dear Lord, why, oh why, did you fashion us so very different from each other?

Well, needless to say we moved to Cote-Saint-Jean in the summer of 1677. Our home sits on a lovely knoll overlooking the St. Lawrence River which gives it an imposing presence. Our land appears to be very fertile and should produce abundant crops with the gift of God's rain. The children are adjusting to the move splendidly and that is the most important thing to me. So I'm content, especially now that our church is almost finished, for when it is completed then I will know I'm home.

On March 13, 1678 Honoré attended the blessing of our L'Enfant Jesus stone church by Monsigneur Lefebvre, Superior of the Seminary and Vicar General, assisted by Monsieur le cure Sequenot and Monsieur Jean Cavalier, frère de sieur La Salle.

As we celebrate little Andre's third birthday I realize we are expecting a baby once again. This time I have a feeling it is a girl. Honoré has no preference now but of course he postscripts his desire with "Please, dear Lord, may the new little one be healthy!"

A precious little girl we name Francoise arrives during our first blizzard of the fall on November 20, 1678. We decide to delay her baptism until the twenty-seventh at our new L'Enfant Jesus Church. The senior Church warden Francois Bau is her Godfather and Francoise Guile, the wife of Andre Traiau is her

Godmother. I believe Sainte-Francois of Assisi will definitely be her Patron Saint.

# CHAPTER 43   HOUSE OF TEARS

Twelve years later, in the dead of the night in April 1691 our house is awakened by the church bells pealing constantly in alarm. Honoré and I leap out of bed to rouse our four children: Anne-Thérèse 22, Jean 19, Andre 16 and Francoise 13 all wrapped up in their blankets as we dash out the back door to the barn to release our terrified horses and cow.

We see with horror that the Iroquois have torched our entire town of thirty homes from one end to the other. It wasn't enough for them that on July second of last year they killed six of our brave men. Honoré shepherds all six of us into our underground root cellar and bolts the door securely. It is obvious to him there is no point in even trying to douse the flames. We huddle here trembling and praying fervently for the safety of our married children and grandchildren who live in their homes across town: Jeanne, who married Joseph Loiselle in '82 have five wonderful children, Marie who married Antoine Villedieu in '85 have one little girl and Marguerite and her husband Andre Heneau who were married in '86.

We pray until dawn and the chanting lulls me as I recall all the sorrows that have plagued our house. A few months after Francoise was born my dear friend Renée Loppé died in the frigid winter of '79 at the age of only thirty-four. She and my cousin Jean Valiquet have eight children. On September seventh of the same year Jean was convicted of incest "having had carnal copulation with one of his daughters and for attempting to ravish the other two." This was a first for New France. He appealed the guilty verdict which would have punished him by the "question extraordinaire" to produce a confession and then hanging him in the square of Montréal until dead and in addition all his property would be seized. The Conseil Souverin rejected the appeal, but commuted the sentence to banishment from within a thirty-league radius of the Isle of Montréal for life. I don't care to ever lay eyes on him again. He has brought disgrace upon our entire family.

Two years later I gave birth to a beautiful baby boy we named Antoine. He lived only three short years and passed away on October thirty-first, 1684 which was six months after I gave birth to our sweet Joseph on April twenty-second. Joseph only lived in this world for eight short days. The following year Antoine (the second) was born on June thirtieth, 1685 only to live three short years just as our first Antoine had done. It is a horrendous ordeal to lose three children in four years.

The quantity of tears that we have shed here could have put out the fire that now engulfs our home. The three weddings that we celebrated during the same period and the births of our grandchildren blunted our unrelenting grief, but you never truly recover from losing four irreplaceable sons in a lifetime. We probably do need a fresh start in a new house, our land having been cleansed by fire.

# AFTER WORDS

My seventh great-grandparents, Honoré and Marie, do rebuild and live to see each of their four children that prayed with them in the root cellar marry and go on to have many children. Anne-Thérèse marries Robert Janot dit La Chapelle in 1693. My ancestor Jean, marries Jeanne Gaultier in '98. Francoise marries Louis Beaudry in 1700 and then Andre wed Francoise Bissonet in 1701.

They also live to see the "Great Peace of Montréal of 1701" end the Beaver Wars, when a lasting peace treaty is finally signed with the Native population.

On December eleventh, 1709 Honoré dies at the advanced age of seventy-seven. At his death he was the oldest inhabitant of his beloved L'Enfant Jesus Parish where he served as Senior Churchwarden. Nine years later on January seventh, 1718 my remarkable great-grandmother, Marie Pontonnier went to be with her Sweet Jesus at the age of seventy-five. They were both buried in the church cemetery at Pointe-Aux-Trembles.

Marie's first husband, Pierre Gadois, waited five years to marry again. In 1665 he took "fille du Roi" Jeanne Bénard as his bride who gave him fourteen children, decisively removing any stigma of the curse.

# ACKNOWLEDGEMENTS

I am elated to have had the opportunity to tell the story of this brave couple that I found while researching my family tree. I could not possibly have written this without the help of the amazingly researched book by Peter J. Gagne: Before the King's Daughters   The Filles à Marier (The Marriageable Girls) 1634-1662.

I'm also in debt to the internet which provided occasionally contradicting factoids but on the whole a fascinating glimpse into the history of New France in the 1600s. It provided this disabled sixty-six year old lady the access to information that would have been impossible to compile just twenty years ago.

I can never thank enough my dear husband of forty-seven years, Frank who patiently listened to my chapters as they jelled and typed my manuscript into the computer while offering "a much better word" now and then.

I'm forever in debt to my good friend Wilma Jones who had the unenviable task of proofreading my manuscript as the chapters slowly fell from my brain during the last three years. Thank you so much, Wilma.

I must thank my four children: Charles, William, Angela and Daniel for their love and support during this endeavor.

Thanks to all my friends for their encouragement, especially the members of our charity Knit and Crochet group who cheered my progress. Your friendship is a blessing to me.

A very large thank you to all the readers of this book. I hope you have enjoyed it.

Made in the USA
Charleston, SC
16 November 2014